# Advance Praise

*The Map to Manhood, A Guide for Young Men Growing Up Without a Dad* is an invaluable compass for young men navigating life's journey without the presence of a father figure. As the President of the non-profit organization Standing with Boys, which is committed to empowering and supporting fatherless youth, I wholeheartedly endorse this remarkable book.

Author James Stephenson has crafted a deeply insightful and compassionate guide, addressing the unique challenges faced by young men who grow up without a dad. This book is a beacon of hope, illuminating the path towards self-discovery, resilience, and ultimately, embracing the true essence of manhood.

*The Map to Manhoo*d emphasizes the significance of learning self-discipline, emotional intelligence, and the importance of love in becoming a successful adult man. It encourages young men to determine their own purposes and embrace their unique qualities with confidence.

I commend James for addressing the delicate subject matter with grace and sensitivity. The book not only acknowledges the challenges but also inspires hope and resilience, showing young men that their potential for success, fulfillment, and happiness is limitless, regardless of their past circumstances.

For parents, mentors, and guardians, this book serves as a valuable resource to better understand and nurture young men who lack paternal guidance. It equips them with the knowledge and insight needed to offer meaningful support, shaping a brighter future for the fatherless youth.

As President of Standing with Boys, I recommend this book to all those dedicated to empowering the next generation of strong, resilient, and compassionate young men.

–Patty Liston, President, Standing with Boys

I am honored to endorse *The Map to Manhood*, an essential guide that offers invaluable direction and support for young men facing the challenges of growing up without a father figure. As a former US Congressman, I have witnessed firsthand the impact of absent fathers on our society. This book serves as a beacon of hope and guidance for those navigating the journey to manhood without paternal guidance.

In *The Map to Manhood*, the author demonstrates a profound understanding of the unique hurdles that young men without a father must overcome. With compassion, insight, and practical advice, this book addresses the complex emotions and uncertainties these young men encounter, empowering them to embrace their full potential and find their way in the world.

The author's empathy shines through as they explore the various aspects of manhood that are often influenced by a father's presence: self-esteem, personal responsibility, emotional intelligence, and the ability to form healthy relationships.

*The Map to Manhood* is more than just a self-help book; it is a compassionate companion, providing solace and support to those who might feel lost or adrift due to the absence of a father figure. Through personal anecdotes, advice based on experience, and actionable steps, the book guides young men toward discovering their true potential and becoming positive forces in their own lives and the lives of those around them.

As a public servant who has always prioritized the well-being and future success of our youth, I wholeheartedly recommend The Map to Manhood to parents, mentors, educators, and most importantly, to the young men who stand to benefit from its wisdom. It is my sincere belief that this book will serve as a guiding light, inspiring young men to rise above their circumstances and embrace the limitless possibilities that await them.

In conclusion, *The Map to Manhood* is an essential and timely work, offering vital direction and empowerment to young men who are forging their paths without a paternal figure. I commend the author for his dedication to this important cause and for crafting a book that is sure to leave a lasting, positive impact on the lives of its readers.

–Alan Steelman, Former US Congressman from Texas

# THE MAP TO
# MANHOOD

# THE MAP TO
# MANHOOD

## A GUIDE FOR YOUNG MEN GROWING UP WITHOUT A DAD

JAMES P. STEPHENSON

STEPDAD PRESS

**The Map to Manhood:**
**A Guide for Young Men Growing Up Without a Dad**

Published by Stepdad Press
Brigham City, Utah, U.S.A.

STEPHENSON, JAMES, P. Author
  THE MAP TO MANHOOD
  JAMES P. STEPHENSON

Library of Congress Control Number: 2023914559

ISBN: 979-8-9888155-0-1, ISBN: 979-8-9888155-1-8 (paperback)
ISBN: 979-8-9888155-2-5 (hardcover)
ISBN: 979-8-9888155-3-2 (digital)

**SELF-HELP** / Personal Growth / Self-Esteem #1

**FAMILY & RELATIONSHIPS** / Life Stages / Adolescence #2

**PSYCHOLOGY** / Developmental / Adulthood & Aging #3

Editing: Susan Crossman (crossmancommunications.com)
Editing: Lisa Shrewsberry (getfinelines.weebly.com)
Book Design: Debbie Stratton (designdogstudio.com)
Publishing Management: Susie Schaefer (finishthebookpublishing.com)

QUANTITY PURCHASES: Schools, companies, professional groups, clubs, and other organizations may qualify for special terms when ordering quantities of this title. For information, email info@mystepdad.org.

# Dedication

*To Mark Gould, my "Stepdad."*

*May the love and help
you gave me
be felt by everyone
who reads this book.*

# Disclaimer

This book details the author's personal opinions, and he makes no representations or warranties of any kind with respect to this book or its contents. The statements made in this book are not intended to diagnose, treat, cure, or prevent any condition or unhappiness. They are meant to assist you in navigating your life and not to replace medical care or therapy.

All content is for informational and educational purposes and does not establish any kind of patient/client relationship. The information presented here is not a substitute for any kind of professional advice. Please consult with your own healthcare specialist or other therapist regarding the suggestions and recommendations made in this book. Before you begin any program or change your lifestyle in any way, you should consult your physician or another licensed practitioner to ensure that you are in good health and that the examples contained in this book will not harm you.

Except as specifically stated in this book, neither the author nor the publisher, nor any authors, contributors, or other representatives, will be liable for damages arising out of or in connection with the use of this book.

This is a comprehensive limitation of liability that applies to all damages of any kind, including (without limitation) compensatory; direct, indirect, or consequential damages; loss of data, income, or profit; loss of or damage to property; and claims of third parties.

If you are experiencing severe anxiety and depression or an immediate crisis, please reach out to a mental health professional, crisis center, or hotline.

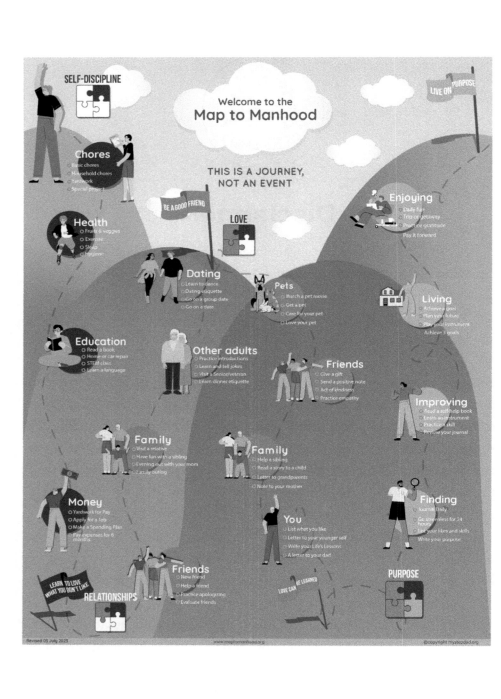

SELF-DISCIPLINE

Welcome to the
**Map to Manhood**

LIVE ON PURPOSE

**Chores**
- Basic chores
- Household chores
- Yardwork
- Special project

THIS IS A JOURNEY,
NOT AN EVENT

BE A GOOD FRIEND

LOVE

**Enjoying**
- Daily fun
- Trip or getaway
- Practice gratitude
- Pay it forward

**Health**
- Fruits & veggies
- Exercise
- Sleep
- Hygiene

**Dating**
- Learn to dance
- Dating etiquette
- Go on a group date
- Go on a date

**Pets**
- Watch a pet movie
- Get a pet
- Care for your pet
- Love your pet

**Living**
- Achieve a goal
- Plan your future
- Play your instrument
- Achieve 3 goals

**Education**
- Read a book
- Home or car repair
- STEM class
- Learn a language

**Other adults**
- Practice introductions
- Learn and tell jokes
- Visit a Senior/veteran
- Learn dinner etiquette

**Friends**
- Give a gift
- Send a positive note
- Act of kindness
- Practice empathy

**Improving**
- Read a self-help book
- Learn an instrument
- Practice a skill
- Review your journal

**Family**
- Visit a relative
- Have fun with a sibling
- Evening out with your mom
- Family outing

**Family**
- Help a sibling
- Read a story to a child
- Letter to grandparents
- Note to your mother

**Finding**
- Journal Daily
- Go screenless for 24 hours
- List your likes and skills
- Write your purpose

**Money**
- Yardwork for Pay
- Apply for a Job
- Make a Spending Plan
- Pay expenses for 6 months

**You**
- List what you like
- Letter to your younger self
- Write your Life's Lessons
- A letter to your dad

LEARN TO LOVE WHAT YOU DON'T LIKE

**Friends**
- New friend
- Help a friend
- Practice apologizing
- Evaluate friends

RELATIONSHIPS

LOVE CAN BE LEARNED

PURPOSE

# Table of Contents

# Introduction

I still remember getting the call from my brother. "Dad passed away today," he said.

I didn't quite know how to feel.

Dad had been declining for a few months. Some days it appeared he wouldn't make it through the night. Then he would rebound and seem better for a few more days. And, while my mind told me I should be sad, my heart still felt some anger and resentment. My conflicted feelings gave rise to a sense of melancholy.

My dad wasn't around when I was born on Christmas Day, 1964. My mom's younger brother drove my mother to the hospital, and I presume my maternal grandparents were home with my four older siblings. I can only imagine how my mother felt. I'm not sure if she realized she was pregnant when she and my father split up. I've subsequently learned that my dad's behavior and attitude changed significantly after they were married, and Mom felt these changes were hurting her and our family. After seeking counseling, she made the difficult decision to separate from—and ultimately divorce—my father.

Growing up without a dad is tough. I had a lot of doubts, concerns, hurt feelings, and even resentment. I couldn't understand how my dad could leave his kids.

When a boy grows up without a dad, some lessons go untaught; some experiences don't happen and, most particularly, the boy doesn't feel the love from a man that he needs.

Children don't reason like adults. Adults are godlike people. In the eyes of a child, adults don't make mistakes. I used to think that if my dad left me, that must mean there was something wrong with me. I would ask myself, "What did I do? What defect do I have that caused my father to leave me?"

As I grew older, the conscious questions changed.

"How am I going to learn to be a good man if my dad's not here to show me how?"

"How can I learn to be a good father when mine isn't here to teach me?"

Today, more children than ever are growing up without the love, guidance, and presence of a dad, but there are also societal challenges that didn't exist when I was growing up fatherless.

There are subtle and occasionally overt messages that can cause a young man to question himself and his worth. They include such ideas as:

- Masculinity is inherently bad.
- Men, by default, have a negative impact on society.
- The world would be better if men played a different role.

Consequently, a fatherless young man today not only has to overcome the self-doubts, fears, and concerns of being fatherless, he must do so in a sea of societal skepticism towards his own masculinity.

> Young men without dads have to overcome self-doubt, fear, and being fatherless, in a sea of societal skepticism towards masculinity.

As an older teenager, I started to wonder how I was going to figure out how to be an adult man. I wanted to have a girlfriend and occasionally did. Eventually, I wanted to get married and have a family of my own, but I worried about what kind of a husband and father I would turn out to be. Fortunately, there were other adult men in my life who were good husbands, good fathers, and good examples to learn from. One, in particular, became a surrogate dad for me. His name was Mark Gould.

Mark was one of our neighbors. He lived around the corner and a few houses down from our home, and he was one of the adult leaders in a group of young men that I became a part of when I turned twelve.

Mark took me under his wing and served as a substitute dad to me, even into adulthood. He took me camping with his family. It was there he taught me to ride motorcycles. He helped me fix the brakes on my mother's car when they needed to be changed. Most of all, Mark loved me. He didn't say, "I love you, Jimmy." Rather, he showed his love to me by spending time with me, helping me, and sometimes by chewing me out. I knew he cared about me and wanted what was best for me.

Mark helped me learn many of the things I otherwise would have struggled to figure out. He didn't have a specific syllabus or course outline. He just let me observe him and spend time with him; occasionally he helped with some of the projects around our home. While Mark didn't have an outlined set of skills intended to help me learn how to be a man, I have since thought a lot about what those skills might be. The Map to Manhood encompasses what I believe are the most important things you need to know to successfully grow into a caring, adult man with integrity.

## The Map to Manhood

The Map to Manhood is a series of actions and activities designed to guide the young man who doesn't have the benefit of a loving in-home father. Four paths make up the journey you are about to take. They are:

- Self-discipline
- Relationships
- Love
- Purpose

Throughout the book there are links to videos from the My Stepdad YouTube channel and other resources addressing the topic at hand. There are also tables and worksheets you can use to track your progress on your journey to manhood, along with places to record your experiences, thoughts, and ideas. I encourage you to wear this book out. Write your thoughts. Record your progress. Keep notes. If you feel inclined, share them with me at dad@mystepdad.org.

You may be a teenage young man with questions like those I had at your age. You may be in your twenties, thirties, or even older, still wondering whether you can figure out how to get over the negative feelings you have about your relationship with your dad.

If you're still hurting or feeling angry at your dad for not being there, then know that you can heal. It doesn't help you to harbor those feelings. It hurts you and those around you by limiting your ability to be the man, husband, and father your future (or current) family deserves.

There is good news. You can break the cycle of fatherlessness. You can heal from the negative emotions you've felt, as well as your own self-doubts and fears. You can be a good man, husband, and father to your own family.

With the help of Mark, my mother, my older siblings, and many others, I managed to learn the things I needed to successfully navigate adulthood. You can, too. I believe the Map to Manhood can help guide you down this path.

Don't expect it to be easy. It takes work and effort over a long period of time, but you will see and feel the changes as you go. Others will see them, too. Probably sooner than you do!

## A Note About the Flow of Your Journey:

This book is presented in sequential order as shown on the Map. You may choose to work on two or three milestones of different segments simultaneously, and not in sequential order. That's okay. I hope you'll choose to complete every milestone. The order is less important, though some actions will build on previous ones.

## Welcome to the Map to Manhood

You can work through this book from start to finish or use this book as a reference manual and work on different sections in accordance with your needs and your situation. Go to whatever set of actions is most relevant for where you are in your life. Each milestone on the Map to Manhood includes actions and activities. Throughout this book you will find worksheets and tables to guide you in completing the actions for each milestone.

You may struggle with some of the actions. I encourage you to do them anyway. Doing difficult or undesirable (but good) things is a sign of maturity, and a skill many adults never acquire. As you travel along your journey to manhood, I hope you will feel my support and encouragement cheering you on along the way.

Let the journey begin!

# SELF-DISCIPLINE

**LEARN TO LOVE WHAT YOU DON'T LIKE**

**Chores**
- Basic chores
- Household chores
- Yardwork
- Special project

**Health**
- Fruits & veggies
- Exercise
- Sleep
- Hygiene

**Education**
- Read a book
- Home or car repair
- STEM class
- Learn a language

**Money**
- Yardwork for Pay
- Apply for a Job
- Make a Spending Plan
- Pay expenses for 3 months

# Path #1:
# Develop Self-Discipline;
# Learning to Love
# What You Don't Like

It happens that my birthday is on Christmas Day and, not surprisingly, Christmas has always been my favorite time of year. As a boy I loved to sit in the living room with only the Christmas tree lights on. The glow they would make as they cast shadows of pine needles on the walls and ceiling was intriguing. I used to take all the presents out from under the tree and then organize them as I put them back.

I would spend time shaking, jiggling, listening to, and trying to guess what the ones that had my name on them were. It was fun to anticipate what they might be, and I looked forward to Christmas morning when I could open the presents and finally enjoy their contents. I was usually excited after I opened them. Occasionally, I was disappointed because I had anticipated something more exciting than the actual present turned out to be.

One year, I was certain that one of my presents was something I really wanted. When I shook it, it sounded just like what I imagined it to be. It was about the right weight and size. I really wanted it. I didn't want to wait for Christmas morning, I wanted it *now*. I must have begged my mom so much that I finally wore her out. She gave me permission to open the present without waiting for Christmas morning.

This was one of those times I was disappointed. It wasn't what I had expected. It was a big letdown. What made it worse was that in my sadness at not getting what I expected, I had disappointed my mother. It was a double disappointment. I didn't get what I wanted, and I had frustrated my mother in the process. She saw my reaction and felt saddened. In that situation, I realized I was disappointed with myself.

Learning to wait for things that we want is an important ability to acquire. We call it "Postponing gratification." It doesn't mean you don't get what you want. It means that sometimes you have to wait for it.

When you have homework that needs to be done and a friend wants to play a game, which would you choose? If there are sweet treats available to you, but you haven't had dinner, do you eat dinner first, or enjoy the treats and then have dinner?

Learning to do the things that are most important *before* you do the things that you want to do is a key to becoming a responsible adult. Many adults never acquire that ability. This doesn't mean you can't have fun or do the things you want to do. It just means that you do them in the proper order. Below are four examples to help you learn to do what is best, *before* doing what you want. These examples will help you learn skills and develop abilities which will help lead you successfully down the road on your journey to manhood. They are:

- Chores
- Health
- Education
- Money

Let's start with chores.

> Postponing gratification
> is learning to wait for
> the things we want in life.

# Milestone #1: Chores

"Chores" is getting to be an old-fashioned term. It means household tasks. We're talking about the things around your home that need to be done for your home to function well.

In my childhood, single-parent household, mom maintained a list of jobs that needed to be done and assigned certain jobs to each of us kids to be completed on a given day of the week. They ranged from sweeping the kitchen to washing the dishes. I don't think she included laundry on the list because it was enough work for her to get us to help with the vacuuming, dusting, making our beds, and cleaning up from meals. The chart looked something like the one below.

In our case, our names were on a row and the tasks we were assigned were in a column with one column for each day of the week. On Wednesdays, I would come home from school, go to the chart, and see what my tasks were for that day. I would begrudgingly go about doing my chores. Washing the dishes was my least favorite. Rinsing and drying wasn't as bad, as it didn't take as long as washing.

If your mom doesn't have a chores chart for you, guess what? You can make your own. Use the example below or download it from www.mystepdad.org/chores. (Yes, this applies to you adult-aged men too. You don't get to skip this part.)

Feel free to modify the chart so that it works for you. It might work best to list all the chores or jobs that need to be done, their frequency, and then write them onto the day during the week that you will complete it. For example, "Make my bed" would be every day but "Clean bedroom" could be once a week on Saturdays.

## Weekly Chores Chart

| Who's Responsible | Sunday | Monday | Tuesday | Wednesday | Thursday | Friday | Saturday |
|---|---|---|---|---|---|---|---|
| [Example] | Make My Bed<br>Take Care of Pet(s) | Make My Bed<br>Do the Dishes<br>Homework | Make My Bed<br>Empty Garbage<br>Homework | Make My Bed<br>Do the Dishes<br>Homework | Make My Bed<br>Dust/Vacuum<br>Homework | Make My Bed<br>Sweep the Floors | Make My Bed<br>Clean My Room<br>Mow the Lawn<br>Homework |
| Me | | | | | | | |
| Mom | | | | | | | |
| Little Sis | | | | | | | |
| | | | | | | | |
| | | | | | | | |
| | | | | | | | |

### Possible Jobs for Your Chart:

| | | |
|---|---|---|
| Walk the dog | Gather laundry | Water the yard |
| Feed the cat/pet | Clear the dinner table | Take out the garbage |
| Water the plants | Mow the lawn | Fix breakfast/lunch/dinner |
| Scoop the catbox | Sweep the kitchen | Clean out a closet/cabinet |
| Do the dishes | Dust and vacuum | Clean the bathroom/shower |

*For downloadable tables and charts, please go to mystepdad.org/resources*

As you put your chores chart together, don't just do it with the jobs that directly affect you. If you live in a house or apartment with other people, you may or may not care if the soap gets refilled in the bathroom or the tub gets cleaned, especially if you never use it. Include those anyway. Most of you reading this will live in a home with other people. In that case, review the cleaning/chores schedule with them and divide the necessary chores among yourselves equitably.

Download the chart and fill it out for your situation. Once you've gotten the chart filled out and printed, hang it in an appropriate place in your home. Ours was in the utility room just off the kitchen. You might want to tape yours to the inside of a pantry door where it is easily accessible, but not always visible.

Make your chart and then live by it for at least one month. In that time, you'll get used to the process, make adjustments and improvements, and hopefully turn it into an ongoing habit.

On the Map to Manhood, you'll notice four types of chores listed. Here are examples of the categories intended for each:

| Basic Chores | Household Chores | Yardwork | Special Project |
|---|---|---|---|
| • Make your bed<br>• Vacuum<br>• Dust<br>• Clean your room<br>• Daily personal hygiene<br>• Daily pet care | • Meal Prep/cooking and Cleanup<br>• Cleaning common areas (living/bathroom/family room, etc.) | • Mow the lawn<br>• Rake leaves<br>• Edge/trim lawn<br>• Apply Fertilizer<br>• Water the lawn | • Interior painting<br>• Home repairs<br>• Home maintenance<br>• Auto maintenance |

Don't get too caught up in the types of chores. Capture all those you can think of initially, put them in the schedule, and start doing them. The biggest benefits of having habits of cleanliness are not just living in a cleaner, nicer home. The biggest benefits will be the pride you will feel in a job well done and the growing confidence you will have as you learn to do hard things first.

## Record your experiences, thoughts, and feelings about this section here:

_____

_____

_____

_____

_____

_____

_____

_____

_____

_____

## Milestone #2: Health & Nutrition

My childhood friend, Danny, started lifting weights when we were teenagers. Since you often do what your friends are doing, I started lifting weights with him. Remember, this was pre-internet time. Danny couldn't do his research on YouTube or search Google. He would get Muscle magazine

and read articles. He started getting protein additives. He even made his own weights by pouring cement into empty coffee cans and embedding an old broom handle into the cement. He mounted pulleys in his garage with cables fixed to homemade weights to use for lat pull-down or triceps extension exercises. One time I remember spotting for him when he was doing bench presses with his homemade barbells, and the broom handle broke mid press. I still remember him saying, "That could have been a disaster." He used the broken weights for the lat pull-down and triceps extension cables.

One year, Danny wanted to host a "Mr. Universe"-type body building contest in his garage. I believe he called it, "Mr. Galaxy." I could never compete with him, but he was going to be a judge, not a contestant. That left me to compete against myself. Not much of a competition.

We finally managed to twist the arm of another of our friends into being in the contest. He happened to be quite a bit taller than I was and, though he was in good shape, I squeaked out the win, earning the title of "Mr. Galaxy" for the only time the competition was ever held. Danny's dad and one of his siblings rounded out the judge's panel.

You may not be ready to win the "Mr. Galaxy" contest in your neighborhood, but how well are you taking care of your body?

What are you doing to make sure it will serve you well through the rest of your life?

Taking care of your body is an important key to successfully growing into manhood.

If you're not already doing this, where can you start? Here are the four areas of this milestone that I recommend you start with:

1. What you eat
2. Physical exercise
3. Sleep
4. Personal hygiene

Let's look at each of these in more detail:

> Your physical body will serve you for the rest of your life. Start now to establish habits to maintain your health.

## 1. What You Eat

You may have noticed when you go to the gas station that there are different grades of fuel. Fuel grades are measured in octane levels. The idea is that the higher-octane fuels are better for your engine.

After I graduated from college, I received a job offer in Michigan. My wife of one-and-a-half years, along with our first child, moved across the country with me as I began a career as a newly minted mechanical engineer in the automotive industry. The first company I worked for made brake and fuel tubing.

I remember I had a conversation with a retired fuel engineer from General Motors who told me that it didn't do a whole lot of good to put premium fuel in a car that had an engine that wasn't designed for it. Some cars are labeled "use only premium unleaded" because those engines are designed for higher octane fuel.

If your body had a fuel label it might say, "Consume only nutritious food." Unfortunately, most of us find that our taste buds often overrule our nutritional wisdom when it comes to what and how much we eat.

Your body is an amazing thing, a miracle, really. It will do the best it can with whatever you put into it. However, if you learn healthy eating habits while you are growing, you will give your body—and you—a much greater advantage for the rest of your life. Even if you are in your forties or fifties, your body will respond positively to nutritional improvements.

So, what are those healthy eating habits?

### A. Don't Overeat

You might be wondering, "How much food is enough, and when should I stop eating?" If you are a teenager and still growing, your body needs more calories than you will need as an adult. One article reports that, on average, teen boys need 2800 calories per day. This can vary significantly based on your height (healthychildren.org).

Tracking your calories to know how much you are getting can be an eye-opening exercise, but most of us aren't likely to do that for a sustained period of time. An easier way to manage how much you eat is by using a scale from 10–0. This idea came from a book I read a while ago, and here's the scale (*The Power of Full Engagement,* by Jim Loehr and Tony Schwartz):

10. Feel sick; hate the thought of food

9. Too full to move

8. Feel sluggish; change into sweats

7. Feel drowsy; unbutton pants; loosen belt

6. Full; feel food in stomach

5. Satisfied; can't feel food in stomach; lasts two-to-three hours

4. Not hungry but not satisfied; hungry within two hours

3. Hungry; stomach growling

2. Grumpy, losing concentration, light-headed

1. Mean, headaches, dizziness

0. So hungry, you aren't hungry anymore

The ideal is that you keep your hunger scale between 3-5 or 3-6. In other words, don't eat until you are so full it slows you down, and don't wait to eat until you're so hungry you're "hangry."

I've been to 10. Trust me, you don't want to go there. It was Thanksgiving. We were celebrating with my in-laws, and there was an abundance of food and dessert. I hadn't yet learned that it is possible to put so much food in your body that it becomes painful. About an hour after dinner, and for what was probably another two or three hours after that, I felt so painfully full that the thought of food was repulsive.

Don't go to 10. Stay at or below 6.

### B. Ensure Fruits and Vegetables Make Up Half of What You Eat

Depending on who does the shopping in your home and what they tend to buy, eating fruits and vegetables may or may not be easy for you. If you fall in the "not easy" category, here is something you can do.

Below are two lists of the most common fruits and vegetables bought in the United States in 2019. Go down each list and make a "+" if you have tried it and like it, and a "-" if you have tried it and don't like it. If you haven't tried it, then try it and decide if you like it or not. I'm including some blank rows at the bottom if you want to add some fruits or vegetables not listed on this chart.

Keep in mind that how food is cooked and seasoned may have an impact on whether you do or do not like it – especially vegetables. You may need to try things in different ways. And don't count French fries as vegetables (though technically they are made from a vegetable). The health factors, if any, are far outweighed by the preparation method. (Deep fried in oil.)

| '+' or '-' | Common Fruits | +' or '-' | Common Vegetables |
|---|---|---|---|
| | Apples | | Potatoes (*not* French Fries!) |
| | Bananas | | Tomatoes |
| | Strawberries | | Onions |
| | Grapes | | Carrots |
| | Oranges | | Broccoli |
| | Watermelon | | Bell Peppers |
| | Avocados | | Lettuce |
| | Peaches | | Cucumbers |
| | Blueberries | | Celery |
| | Pineapples | | Corn |
| | Cantaloupes | | Mushrooms |
| | Cherries | | Cabbage |
| | Pears | | Spinach |
| | Raspberries | | Sweet Potatoes |
| | Plums | | Green Beans |
| | Nectarines | | Cauliflower |
| | | | |
| | | | |
| | | | |
| | | | |
| | | | |

Make sure to include the fruits and vegetables that have a "+" by them on the grocery list next time you go shopping. And get one or two of the ones you have not yet tried to determine which ones you like. Keep in mind that your tastes will change over time. If you tried cauliflower when you were younger and you didn't like it, you might like it now.

### C. Avoid Excess Sweets and Sweet Treats

When I was growing up, we didn't have a lot of candy or sugary, high-calorie, low-nutrition foods in our home. So, whenever I had the chance to get something sweet, it was a real treat. At my friend Danny's house, there was often a bowl of candy or treats on the counter. Since it was such a rarity at our home, I found that I wanted to have as much of it as I could get without being too greedy.

Danny, on the other hand, didn't seem too interested, perhaps because he could have some whenever he wanted. In either case, neither of us overindulged in the sweet treats, though we did enjoy them.

It's okay to have a sweet treat now and again. Even every day if you want. However, if you binge on a bag of candy bars in one-sitting, that may not be a good idea for your overall health.

As an adult, I gained so much weight I had to have my wedding band sized up. Eventually I realized that weight gain was not the inevitable result of growing older. It had never been an issue when I was a young man.

When I decided to do something about it, I started exercising and tracking my calories. I had a calorie budget of around 1800 calories per day. As I entered everything I ate, as well as my exercise (negative calories), I learned where the calories, and therefore the extra weight, was coming from. I learned that a disproportionate amount of my calories came from the sweet treats, not from the vegetables.

Have a treat if you want one, but don't make it the main part of your diet.

## 2. Physical Exercise

When I was between three and five years old, I sometimes fell asleep in my mom's bed. I remember waking up to the sound of her arms slapping against her body as she started her day with jumping jacks. She had understood that it helped her to have regular, daily, physical activity.

As your body is developing, physical activity is especially important. You don't have to go to the gym and become a body builder to be physically fit. Unless you have a job that requires physical labor, you will need to exercise to help your body develop well.

Here is the simple exercise routine that I have evolved to in my adult life:

### Three sets each of
- Push-ups
- Planks
- Squats or Lunges

In adulthood, I got out of the habit of exercising. When I started to pay more attention to my eating and my physical shape, I started doing push-ups. At first, I couldn't do very many. As I kept doing it, I could do more.

Push-ups primarily work your pectoral (chest) muscles and your triceps. I also wanted to work on my stomach muscles, so I started doing sit-ups. After years of doing sit-ups, I've switched to planks. Planks work more of your core muscles than sit-ups do, and I've learned that sit-ups can sometimes be bad for your back and neck.

For quite a while, all I did was push-ups and sit-ups, until my son Wesley said I should add squats to get some lower body muscles into my routine. So, I added squats. He was right. I immediately felt sore in my quads and hamstrings (the upper leg muscles on the front and back of your legs).

One reason I like this simple set of three exercises is that none of them require any special equipment. You don't need weights. You don't have to go to a gym. You can do them at home in your bedroom, or wherever you happen to be. (On a long flight from Europe once, I went to the back galley of the airplane and did push-ups at 30,000 ft.!)

## Running with Wesley

My son Wesley took an interest in physical exercise and downloaded an app that helped him start running. He gradually increased his distance as he persisted in his new exercise routine.

One day he said, "Dad, you should come running with me." I hadn't ever been running, but I thought, "What the heck, I'll give it a shot."

The next time Wesley went running, I went with him. We had run maybe half a block and I said, "I've got to stop."

Wesley is always very positive and encouraging, and he graciously stopped. We walked until I had caught my breath enough to run a bit more. I felt bad for slowing him down, as I could only manage some short stints of running, followed by stretches of walking to recover.

But guess what? As I persisted, I got to where I didn't need to take walking breaks in between running stints. It wasn't easy, and I had to push

*With my son Wesley at a fun run*

myself. I would look ahead and pick out a parked vehicle and say, "I can make it to there, and then I'll walk if I have to." Sometimes I would walk once I got to the vehicle, and sometimes I chose to keep running to the next visual milestone. Eventually, I got to where I could run without stopping.

For "fun" one year, Wes and I entered a local 5K race. It was rewarding to be able to complete the race together, though we were in different age brackets.

In addition to the push-ups, planks, and squats, it would be good for you to add some cardiovascular exercise to your routine. In fact, it's not a bad practice to alternate days. You could do something like this:

Monday, Wednesday, and Friday:      *Strength exercises*
Tuesday, Thursday, and Saturday:     *Go running*
Sunday:                              *Take the day off*

When my mother was dying of cancer, it was my privilege, along with some of my siblings, to stay in her home, care for her, and be with her until the day she passed away. One night, two days before her heart stopped beating, I walked into her room. She had her arms up as she lay in bed. I gently asked her, "Mom, what are you doing?" Her one-word reply was, "Exercise." I said to my dying mother, with all the love I was feeling for her,

"You can exercise tomorrow, Mom. Why don't you put your hands down and rest for now?"

Exercise was one of the earliest examples of positive behavior I remember from my mother. It was also the last word I heard her say.

Whatever exercise schedule you make for yourself, do it. It is a step in the direction of manhood. Take the step!

## My Exercise Routine:

If you don't have an exercise routine, you can start with "Stepdad's" exercise schedule. You'll need to determine how many push-ups, squats, and lunges you want to do, and how long you are going to plank. If you're just starting, it may not be much, but the more you do it, the easier it will become. You can add to your number of reps as your physical ability increases.

Adjust your workout routine as needed. Try different exercises. Find what works for you, but make sure you are exercising regularly.

| Exercise | Sun | Mon | Tues | Wed | Thurs | Fri | Sat |
|---|---|---|---|---|---|---|---|
| Push Ups | | 3 sets | Off | 3 sets | Off | 3 sets | Off |
| Planks | | 3 sets | Off | 3 sets | Off | 3 sets | Off |
| Squats/ Lunges | | 3 sets | Off | 3 sets | Off | 3 sets | Off |
| Running | | Off | Run | Off | Run | Off | Run |
| | | | | | | | |
| | | | | | | | |

## 3. Sleep

Your body is not a machine. And although even machines need maintenance to function properly, machines don't need sleep. Your body does. In fact, sleep is one of the most important ways to "maintain" your body. Studies have compared the impact changing a behavior has on how much longer it will help you live, and they have found that getting more sleep is more important than improving what you eat (Harvard Business Review, Tony Schwartz).

You may be tempted to stay up late doing things you enjoy, past the time when it would be better for you to go to bed. Sleeping on a schedule helps ensure the quality of your sleep is at its best.

In my later years in high school, when I was the only child at home, I developed the habit of going to bed early, by choice. The local radio station had a program they would broadcast every weeknight at 8:00 p.m., called "Radio Mystery Theater." I would go to bed at that time, set my "sleep timer" on my alarm clock radio for sixty minutes, and go to sleep listening to voice actors create a story which formed its image in my mind as I drifted off to sleep.

Going to bed at 8:00 p.m. allowed me to get a good night's sleep and then get up early. After I woke up, I would fix my own breakfast of bacon, eggs, and toast, take our dog for a run (with me on my bike and him on a long leash), and then ride my bike a few miles to school.

You may not naturally be a morning person. And you may not choose to go to bed at 8:00 p.m. That's okay. But going to bed earlier and getting between eight and nine hours of sleep each night will allow you to stay in a better mood, think more clearly, and do better physically than if you try to function on less sleep.

Try it and see what you think from your own experience, but don't just try it for a night. Do it for a week or more before you draw your own conclusions.

> Good sleep is one of the most important ways to maintain a healthy body and mind.

## My Map to Manhood Sleep Tracker

Use the charts below to log your sleep times for two weeks.

| Week 1 | Sun | Mon | Tue | Wed | Thu | Fri | Sat |
|---|---|---|---|---|---|---|---|
| In bed (lights out) | | | | | | | |
| Wake up time: (out of bed) | | | | | | | |
| Total Hours Slept: | | | | | | | |

| Week 2 | Sun | Mon | Tue | Wed | Thu | Fri | Sat |
|---|---|---|---|---|---|---|---|
| In bed (lights out) | | | | | | | |
| Wake up time: (out of bed) | | | | | | | |
| Total Hours Slept: | | | | | | | |

Look for patterns and shoot for a regular schedule. Make sure you're getting enough sleep every night.

## 4. Personal Hygiene

One day at work, after making a presentation to a group of people, my boss called me into his office. That can be concerning. In this case, he said, "Some of the people notice that you are putting your hands in your pockets and 'adjusting things' when you're in front of everybody."

He was quite gracious in helping me understand that although I thought this habit was a casual, subtle, and an unnoticeable action, it wasn't to anyone else watching me!

Sometimes my man parts get sweaty and sticky. Especially when I'm in front of an audience. In my mind, with my hand inside my pocket, no one could see that I was peeling my man parts away from my inner thigh to give it a breath of fresh air between my legs. My boss suggested I start using powder on my private parts going forward.

That's a bit embarrassing to admit, but I'm grateful for that lesson learned. I've been powdering my privates ever since, and crotch sweat is largely a thing of the past.

This is an example of personal hygiene. For most of us, taking care of our physical appearance, including grooming, showering, and keeping our clothes clean, happens naturally as our social interactions increase. We don't want to be smelly or look stupid or unkempt. When we start taking an interest in the opposite sex, we become even more conscious of the need to take care of our personal hygiene. What does that mean?

**Here are the basics of personal hygiene:**
- Brush your teeth twice daily (gum or mints can help during the day)
  - o Floss daily
- Take a shower/bath daily
  - o Shampoo your hair
  - o Soap your body
- Shave
- Use deodorant
  - o Powder your privates (optional, but recommended)
  - o Apply cologne (also optional)
- Wear clean, matching clothes

If the above items are not habits for you, work to make them so. If you need help making them habits, here is a chart you can use to help you develop these habits:

| Action | Sun | Mon | Tue | Wed | Thu | Fri | Sat |
|---|---|---|---|---|---|---|---|
| Brush teeth (2x) | | | | | | | |
| Floss | | | | | | | |
| Shower/bath | | | | | | | |
| Shave | | | | | | | |
| Deodorant/cologne | | | | | | | |
| Clean clothes | | | | | | | |

On the self-discipline track, the above areas will do much to help you gain confidence and feel better about yourself physically. You may not expect it, but they will have a significant impact on your emotional well-being, too.

You'll be proving to yourself that you can care for yourself. If all these things (exercise, nutrition, sleep, and hygiene) are more than you're ready to take on all at once, start with one until it gets easier, then add the next and so on. You can do it.

## Record your experiences, thoughts, and feelings about this section here:

_____

_____

_____

_____

_____

_____

_____

_____

_____

_____

# Milestone #3: Education - Mind Your Mind

Feeding yourself the right amount of good food is essential to having a healthy body. Feeding your mind is even more important! Here's the deal with "mental nutrition": you're feeding your mind whether you're aware of it or not.

I doubt it will ever happen, but can you imagine someone running up to you and shoving a donut in your mouth? Yet that happens every day with what ends up going into your mind.

One day during grade school when I was sitting with my friends waiting for our turn to get lunch, one of my friends unfolded a piece of paper and handed it to me. On it was a picture of a naked lady, stretched out on a lounge chair. That was more than forty years ago, and I still remember it. When it comes to "mental nutrition" it may be much easier for someone to come and shove a donut in your mouth. But always remember this: you get to choose what you feed your mind.

If you take a passive approach to this issue—or the easy path—you'll probably spend a lot of time watching funny cat videos or scrolling through whatever funny video or meme is going around the internet on any given day. Choosing to view pornography or violent videos or listening to excessively foul language is not much different from smoking or using addictive drugs in terms of the damage it does. What you watch and listen to can range from a healthy mental diet to a junk food diet to a toxic diet. Be careful with your choices. Your mental nutrition has significant consequences for good or bad.

If you want to give yourself a healthier "mental" diet, then you can choose what you put in front of your eyes, and into your ears.

We've already established that when I was in high school, I was a little different than other kids. As I was going to sleep at night, I would listen to cassette tapes of motivational talks and stories. Once, as an older teenager, I was in my front yard washing my mom's car while listening to a motivational tape on my "boom box." An older friend of mine, who had a year or two of college under her belt, came by on her bicycle. She stopped and chatted for a bit. When she heard what I was listening to, she told me I might want to reconsider. "People that listen to motivational stuff often get depressed," she said. Why was that? "Because they never meet their own standard."

She was a psychology major.

Despite my friend's warning, to this day I believe feeding your mind positive thoughts and inspiring stories of others' achievements can inspire and motivate you. Many of today's respected speakers have found their "purpose" and want to share their stories and uplift others. However, great motivational talks are not the only way to feed yourself good mental nutrition. Completing your school studies, with the intent of truly understanding the concepts, not just passing tests to get good grades—is another way.

Whenever your body is busy, such as when you exercise or mow the lawn, often your mind is not. During that busy time, you can choose what you feed your otherwise idle mind. It could be good music, an audiobook, a motivational talk from someone you admire, or something entertaining or educational. Choose what you feed your mind carefully and deliberately.

> Choose wisely. What you feed your mind is as important as what you feed your body.

Here are some actions and activities that will help you develop your mental capacities:

## 1. Read a book that has more than 100 pages

When I was in my early twenties, a friend of mine told me how much he was enjoying a book he was reading. He said, "Get anything by Tom Clancy." I had finished college, was newly married and didn't have college studies to deal with, so I got a book by Tom Clancy. As I started reading it, I got so into the book that I didn't want to put it down.

When you find a book that interests you, reading is not only easy, but almost addictive. Reading just for reading's sake may not be a bad thing, especially as an alternative to mindless scrolling or social media, but it becomes even more valuable when it educates you in the process.

I enjoy reading biographies and history books. Historical novels can both entertain and educate.

Whatever genre you enjoy, find a book and read it. My practice for years has been to read for 15-30 minutes after getting in bed for the night. Taking a book in the bathroom is also a much better alternative than your phone.

## 2. Do a home maintenance or auto repair project

What is there around your home that needs to be fixed? Or is there something wrong with your vehicle that needs to be repaired? You can watch all the YouTube videos in the world, and you might know a lot more, but until you've done something you won't have learned it. YouTube and the internet are great ways to figure things out. Most of us learn quicker when we can see something rather than have it explained to us. So, figure out how to fix that squeaky door, or patch a hole in the wall, or change the brakes, or whatever project would benefit from your efforts.

## 3. Complete a class in a Science, Technology, Engineering or Math (STEM) topic

I paid a lot of money to get my college engineering degree. It wasn't always easy. Some classes were harder than others. Modern Physics was the most difficult for me personally, but with the help of occasional tutors, teacher office hours, fellow students, and persistence, I was finally able to graduate.

You don't need to get a college degree to meet this milestone action, but I do want you to take a STEM related class and finish it. At the time of this writing there are numerous free online options available. Here are some that you can look into, or search for other options, including paid courses.

- Khan Academy: https://www.khanacademy.org/
- Coursera: https://www.coursera.org/
- MIT OpenCourseWare: https://ocw.mit.edu/index.htm

- Harvard University's Online Learning: https://online-learning. harvard.edu/
- OpenLearn: https://www.open.edu/openlearn/
- UC Berkeley Webcasts: https://webcast.berkeley.edu/
- Saylor Academy: https://www.saylor.org/

Whatever level of math or other STEM class you choose to take, find the next level higher and take it.

## 4. Learn a second language

I took two years of Spanish in high school. I was surprised that when I began learning a second language, I understood things about my native language. Conjugating verbs finally made sense. I didn't know what an infinitive form of a verb was because in English there had never been a need for me to understand it. In Spanish it became clear as the base verb is presented in the infinitive form and then conjugated, or put in the proper form, based on whether I was doing it, you were doing it, or someone else was doing it. It gets even more fun if it was something you did in the past, or something we planned to do in the future.

Learning a second language can seem intimidating, unless you've grown up in a bilingual home or community, but it has tremendous benefit intellectually. As with the online education options listed above, there are also free learning tools that can make the process fun. In the chart below I have listed some of them. I have used Duolingo to study German for a few years during the time my daughter and her family lived in Germany. I only made it over twice, but it helped tremendously to be able to communicate even basic sentences when needed. Besides, if my five-year-old granddaughter could learn German, it seemed like I should be able to too.

# Record your experiences, thoughts, and feelings about this section here:

_____

_____

_____

_____

_____

_____

_____

_____

_____

_____

## Self-discipline—Milestone #3: "Education" Actions

| Action | Date Completed | Explanation | Examples/ Options |
|---|---|---|---|
| Read a book that has more than 100 pages | | Reading a book can be as engaging, sometimes addictive, as video games, when you get the right book. Here are some examples of books and authors, but there are too many to list. Find one you like and read it. | • Michael Vey Series<br>• The Candy Shop Wars<br>• Tom Clancy<br>• Biographies<br>• History books or historical novels |
| Do maintenance or make a needed vehicle or home repair | | Learn a new skill such as how to change your own oil, replace a burned-out light bulb in a car or light fixture, fix a leak, replace a faucet, or do some other vehicle or home repair. | • Search online for "How-to" videos (Check out the My Stepdad YouTube channel for many examples)<br>• Ask a friend or neighbor for help |
| Find an online class about STEM and complete it | | There are many online options for self-education. If you've made it through trigonometry in math, then learn algebra. Choose at least one course in Science, Technology, Engineering or Math (STEM) and complete it. | • Khan Academy<br>• Coursera<br>• MIT<br>• Harvard<br>• Open Learn<br>• Berkley<br>• Saylor<br>• Udemy.com<br>• Edx.org |
| Study a different language daily for at least 6 weeks. | | Learning a different language has many benefits. You'll understand your native language better. Numerous online and mobile apps facilitate language learning – I'm sure you can find one that works well for you. | • Duolingo<br>• Babbel<br>• Search online<br>• Google Translate |

# Milestone #4: Manage Your Money

When I was fourteen or fifteen years old, a man I knew told me that his boss was looking for someone to do some small projects at his work for pay. I would have much preferred to stay home and watch TV, but I knew it was better to go out and earn some money, so I said I would do it. After all, it was only for a few projects over a couple of days.

On the third day of working on various handyman jobs, I was standing on the roof of a building working on some swamp coolers when my friend called to me and said, "Hey, Jimmy. Good news! He wants to make it a permanent part-time job."

My heart sank. I figured I could do this for a couple of days, but to have to go to work for four or five hours every day didn't excite me.

Until I got my paycheck.

I think I was earning $3.50 an hour, but the hours added up, and things didn't cost as much back then. When I got a paycheck, I suddenly had options. I remember one of the first purchases I made for myself was a book from the National Geographic Foundation called, "America's Wonders." It was only $15 but I wanted it, and I had the money to buy it without asking my mom for it. I still have that book.

My own money gave me a new level of independence.

What can you do to start, or increase, the amount of income you have? There are a lot of ways people can earn money. Working for a local business or other company may be the most common and easiest way to do that, but a lot of people have started their own businesses and succeeded.

*Figure 1. Scan this to see an interview with a professor of entrepreneurship.*

Whatever you do, take action to start earning an income.

Because I had been raised in frugal circumstances, I was naturally cautious about spending money. However, when I had enough money to buy my own stereo system, I went to the downtown department store and looked through their stereo selection. I finally settled on a record player, a radio tuner, and a cassette player console. The speakers that came with it were stand-alone right and left speakers that you connected by wires into the back of the console. It cost me a little over $200. In the early '80s that was a big investment for me!

Unfortunately, they didn't have any in stock. They only had the display unit. The salesman said he could order it in, and I would have it in about a week. I went home excited about my new purchase.

Have you ever heard of buyer's remorse? Not long after I got home, I got worried about spending that much money on a stereo, I started questioning whether that was the right thing to do. I second-guessed myself so much that after a couple of days, I called the store and told them to cancel my order. A few days later, I regretted backing out. You guessed it, I called the store and asked them if they could still bring it in.

I got the stereo.

You may not have the same worries about spending money, but either way it's important to remember that for you to be successful as an adult, you need to be responsible when it comes to taking care of your money.

You need to earn it, and you need to use what you earn responsibly.

Here is a simple formula that you can use to help you stay on track.

For every dollar you earn, live on 70 cents. So, what happens to the other 30 cents?

- Give 10% to charity
- Save 10%
- Invest 10%

If you are doing those three things with the first 30 cents of every dollar you make, you will be financially well set up for your future.

Minding your money well is a step in the direction of manhood.

Take the step!

Here is a worksheet to help you succeed in managing your money. (For more detailed information about setting up and tracking a monthly spending plan, see my previous book, "Small Steps, Big Feat". www.smallstepsbigfeat.com)

## One-Page Monthly Spending Plan

**Planned Income:**                                          Month: _____

Salary. _____
Investment. _____
Other. _____
Total Planned Income. _____      10% = _____

**Planned Spending:**                                       **Percentage:**

**Auto:** Auto Insurance. _____     _____
**Auto:** Payment. _____     _____
**Auto:** Gas & Fuel. _____     _____
**Auto:** Service & Parts. _____     _____
**Bills & Utilities:** Internet. _____     _____
**Bills & Utilities:** Mobile phone. _____     _____
**Bills & Utilities:** Utilities. _____     _____
**Education:** *Personal Dev.* _____     _____
**Financial:** *Active Investments.* _____     10%
**Financial:** Life Insurance. _____     _____
**Financial:** *Passive Investments.* _____     10%
**Food:** Fast Food. _____     _____
**Food:** Groceries. _____     _____
**Food:** Restaurants. _____     _____
**Gifts & Donations:** *Charity.* _____     10%
**Gifts & Donations:** Gifts. _____     _____
**Health:** Doctor/Dentist. _____     _____
**Health:** Medical Insurance. _____     _____
**Health:** Medicine. _____     _____
**Home:** Insurance. _____     _____
**Home:** Mortgage & Rent. _____     _____
**Home:** Maintenance. _____     _____
**Kid's:** Babysitter & Daycare. _____     _____
**Kids:** Kids Activities. _____     _____
**Miscellaneous** Expenses. _____     _____
**Shopping:** Clothing. _____     _____
**Transfer:** To Cash for Spending. _____     _____
**Travel:** Vacation. _____     _____

Total Planned Spending. _____     _____

## Self-Discipline—Milestone #4: "Manage Your Money" Actions

| Action | Date Completed | Explanation | Examples/ Options |
|---|---|---|---|
| Do yardwork for a neighbor for pay | | Look around your neighborhood and ask yourself who you think would be willing to pay you to do some yardwork. If you're past the age where you think this is appropriate, think about starting your own lawncare business. | • Mow a lawn<br>• Edge a lawn<br>• Shovel snow<br>• Paint house numbers on curbs |
| Apply for a job | | Starting out, one of the scarier things you may face is applying for your first job. If you haven't done so yourself, talk to a friend who has done it and ask what they did.<br><br>You can do it. As scary as it might seem, think about how nice it will be having money coming in. | • Local fast-food restaurant<br>• Grocery store<br>• Search jobs near you online<br>• Create/update your resume or CV |
| Establish a monthly spending plan and stick to it for 3 months | | Using the template above, determine how much you anticipate making this month. Calculate 10% of that income and plan to save, invest, and donate 10% to each of those categories and live on the remaining 70%. Make a new spending plan each month for 3 months. | • Create a spending plan at the beginning of the month<br>• Track it weekly<br>• You may have to adjust, but do so only when necessary<br>• Do it again next month |
| Work at one job for 6 months or earn money to pay your own expenses for 6 months. | | As you start working, it is important that you work to be a good employee. Be consistent in your attendance. Do a good job every time you work. This is not just so that you will be looked at as a good employee, but it is especially important for you to prove to yourself that you can be a responsible person. | • Be consistent in your attendance<br>• Do good work each time you work<br>• Look for ways to improve as a worker |

# Record your experiences, thoughts, and feelings about this section here:

_____

_____

_____

_____

_____

_____

_____

_____

_____

_____

_____

Success as an adult
is directly impacted with
how you choose to be
responsible for your money.

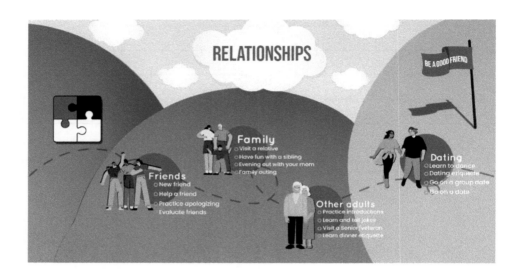

# Path #2:
# Develop Healthy Relationships

My grandma lived in the small farming town where my mom had been raised. One weekend when I was a teenager, my family went to visit my grandmother. I happened to be the only one in the house one morning when a knock came at the door. A neighbor lady, whom I didn't know, wanted to drop something off for my grandmother.

I wasn't always gracious in my interactions with people in those days, but this time, I told the neighbor how thoughtful she was, and I assured her I would get the item to my grandmother. I told her I was sure my grandmother would be very pleased.

As it turned out, this neighbor ran into my mother and aunt later. She told them of the positively charming young man she had met at Macel's (my grandmother's) house. The experience taught me that one of the most valuable skills you can acquire is the ability to positively interact with other people. You can

> Social skills are valuable for interpersonal relationships as well as professional communication.

be the smartest person around, but if you're a jerk everyone will know it, and no one will want to work with you, for you, or around you. On the other hand, as you develop the ability to positively work with other people, you will become of greater service and value to the people you work for, more so than someone who may be technically skilled but is not good at working with people.

Let's look at ways you can develop your social skills. We'll start with your friends.

## Milestone #5: Friends

The best way to have good friends is to be one. Here are some simple guidelines to show you what I mean:

### 1. When your friend needs something, help them.

When I was the last child at home, there was one family car available. It was a Chevy Malibu Classic. I had a date planned one Saturday night, and my mom knew I needed the car. She assured me that she would be home by the time I needed to leave, but she forgot. (Moms are human, too.)

Earlier that day I had been out with my friend, Lynn, who had his own car. I believe it was a Chevy Chevelle. Lynn took excellent care of his car,

You will notice that "Friends" and "Family" come up in two places on the Map to Manhood. One is in relationships, with a focus on developing social skills, while the other is on the path of Love, with a focus on learning to genuinely feel and appropriately express love

regularly washing and waxing it. His dad owned an auto repair shop, so he took great care of it mechanically, too. I mentioned to him when we were together that if mom didn't get home in time, I might not have a car to go on my date. He said, "If she doesn't get home, then give me a call."

When the time approached that I should be leaving and my mom was nowhere in sight, I took Lynn up on his offer and gave him a call. It's times like these when you find out if someone is just saying something or if they actually mean what they say. (These were pre-cell phone days, where calling someone was from one house phone to another.) Lynn came over with his car, had me drop him back off at his house, and let me take his car on my date.

Benjamin Franklin coined the phrase, "A friend in need, is a friend indeed." I didn't understand what that meant until I was in need, and my friend came through.

When you find that one of your friends has a need and you are in a position to help them, do it. Not only will they forever be appreciative, but you will also feel better about yourself. Someday you will likely be the friend "in need" and hopefully you'll have a friend that is willing to help you out.

## 2. Express your friendship to your friend.

When you're having a good time with your friends, don't be afraid to express it. Saying something like, "I'm glad we're friends," or "I enjoy doing things together," may seem strange to you, but I encourage you to find an appropriate way to express your friendship to your friends.

As boys and men, sometimes we tend to communicate affection through sarcasm. Saying something derogatory but with a smile may be one way of expressing friendship and affection, and it can be appropriate, so long as you are both on the same wavelength.

On the other hand, sarcasm can be negative if you are hurting the person you are talking with or using it to chip away at their self-confidence. Before cracking a joke or being sarcastic, put yourself in your friend's shoes: would you feel better or worse if you were on the receiving end of your comment?

As an example: One day, one of my friends said something sarcastically to me as a joke. I laughed, but his comment stung. I know he didn't intend to hurt my feelings, but he did. It wasn't until later when we were communicating more openly that I told him his previous comment had hurt my feelings. He hadn't realized that and quickly apologized.

My friend's apology leads us to #3 on our list—apologize.

## 3. Apologize when you've said or done something that might have hurt someone.

When my friend genuinely apologized, I felt like our relationship had healed. We have lived for decades beyond our Junior High and High School years and have kept in touch off and on since then. I believe our friendship was preserved and strengthened because he was gracious enough to apologize, and I was happy to let go of my hurt.

You may or may not keep in touch with your friends from your teenage years after high school when your paths take you in different directions, but always be the kind of friend people would want to have for life.

There are challenges to having friends today—such as cell phones, social media, and the internet—that I didn't experience when I was growing up. You may feel like you have friends because you message them online. Indeed, you can connect with people in ways that weren't available when I was growing up. However, your opportunities to develop deeper friendships will be limited if you don't do things together in person as well. Don't just chat, connect, and play video games online. Invite your friends over to hang out together to watch a movie, play soccer or basketball, ride bikes, or whatever else you may have in common. Go to their homes, as well. Let them get to know your parents and family members. Get to know theirs. Talking face to face will allow you to get to know people on a deeper level and help them get to know you, too.

## 4. Choose your friends carefully.

I want to add a caution about friends. Good friends help you be your best. If the friends you have chosen are not doing that, then choose other friends. Trust me when I tell you that it can make a world of difference to your future.

Ask yourself this: "Are my friends helping or hurting me?" You can't expect perfection from friends, any more than you can of yourself, but your friends are having a much bigger influence on you than you realize. You're probably dressing like they dress, adopting ideas that they talk about, going to places they go to, and so on.

That can be good or bad, depending on how they are dressing, what they're talking about, and where they're going. If you were to make a list of your friends and decide whether you are better, the same, or worse when you are around them than when you are not around them, what would your list look like?

If you spend your time with people who are bringing out the worst in you, you need new friends. You don't have to announce to them, "I'm not going to hang out with you anymore because you're a bad influence on me." Just start choosing to fill your time and availability with those who help you be your best self. In the example above, you would be better to quit hanging around with Ethan and Alexander and spend more time with Jacob and Logan.

| Friend | Better (+), Same (=) or Worse (-) |
|--------|-----------------------------------|
| Jacob | |
| Ethan | |
| Alexander | |
| Logan | |
| Jack | |

*Figure 2. Scan this to watch Stepdad talk about choosing your friends wisely.*

# Healthy Relationships—Milestone #5: "Socializing with Friends" Actions

| Action | Date Completed | Explanation | Examples/Options |
|---|---|---|---|
| Make a new friend | | If you have made a new friend in the last 6 months, go ahead and count that. If you haven't, then find a new friend. | Could meet them through:<br>• School<br>• Work<br>• Your Neighborhood |
| Help a friend in need | | As in the story above where Lynn loaned me his car on the spur of the moment, pay attention to your friends. When you see a need they may have, offer to help them with it. | • Listen to them<br>• Help with their yard/ housework |
| Apologize when you should | | Seldom do we have a relationship with a friend when we don't say or do something we later regret. When that happens, apologize. | Potential Events:<br>• You say something that turned out to be rude or hurtful<br>• You say something unkind about your friend to someone else<br>• Didn't follow through with something you said you would do |
| Evaluate the influence of your friends on you, and choose those who are positive | | Do the exercise described above evaluating the friends that you spend the most time with.<br><br>| Friend | +/=/- |<br>\|---\|---\|<br>\| \| \|<br>\| \| \|<br>\| \| \|<br>\| \| \| | Do this periodically (every 6 months to a year)<br><br>Make sure you are a positive influence on your friends, too! |

# Record your experiences, thoughts, and feelings about this section here:

## Milestone #6: Family

As with our "Friends" discussion we are going to come across "Family" on two paths on the journey to manhood. While there is synergy between the two milestones, this one focuses on developing positive

relationships with members of your family. (On the "Love" path, we'll look more at developing a healthy love for our family members.)

Not long ago, two of my sons bought motorcycles. One of the neat things about motorcycles is that as soon as you are a motorcycle rider, you belong to a group. If you pay attention when you're on the road and you see one motorcycle passing another going a different direction, the riders give each other the "Biker wave." In other words, they extend their left hands down and out as they pass each other.

Occasionally I'll borrow one of my son's motorcycles and go for a ride. When I do, I always hope to pass another biker, just so I can give him or her the biker wave.

It feels good to belong.

Your family and extended family constitute one of the groups you belong to. You belong to it because of the relationships you have with the people in it, and these provide opportunities for you to develop socially. Let's look at some of those opportunities.

### Extended Family

If you're lucky enough to live near any cousins, aunts, or uncles, then make sure you do fun things with them. One of my aunts and her husband lived for a time in the same small farming community as my grandmother while my siblings and I were growing up. One of the best parts of visiting Grandma was getting to hang out with my cousins. We would go fishing up the canyon or shoot their .22 rifle at the junk yard. We often just played card games together. We also worked together.

What can you do with your cousins, aunts, or uncles that will bring you closer together?

As you make the effort to be involved with your extended family, you will feel a greater sense of belonging. In the table at the end of this milestone are some suggested activities for you to do with members of your extended family. If you haven't done any of them, make it a point to start. Don't be constrained by the suggestions. If you have something else you would like to do with your extended family members, then go for it.

## Your Siblings

There were two trees in the front yard of our childhood home and another in the strip of lawn between the sidewalk and the street. At the end of the strip was a telephone pole. My older brothers and sisters would sometimes get together in the evenings, preferably after dark, and play "Hide and Go Seek." On a good night, we could attract a big bunch of friends. Whoever was "It" would hide their face in their elbow, lean against the telephone pole, count to twenty, and then shout, "Ready or not, you shall be caught." After that, they would go searching for everyone who was hiding.

Those in hiding would try to get back to the telephone pole without being detected by whoever was "It" for the round. But if the person who was "It" found us in our hiding place, then it was a race back to the telephone pole. If "It" got there first, they would shout, "1, 2, 3 on Jimmy" (or whoever they had seen), and then touch the telephone pole before the person hiding made it back to the telephone pole. The last person who was caught would be "It" for the next round.

This is just one example of an activity that my siblings and I did together when we were growing up. Unless you are an only child, you have a brother or sister. If you don't, then hopefully you have a friend who has siblings. Perhaps those relationships can help you with this section if needed.

What opportunities do you have for doing things with your siblings? Maybe you could have a "Sibling Night" where you play card games together, or watch a family movie, or put together a puzzle. See what everyone would like to do, then do it.

Now that our children are all adults, it has been very rewarding for my wife and me to see them interact together as friends. They don't always agree. They certainly didn't always get along when they were growing up, but they have learned to be friends in adulthood.

Find a fun activity you can do with your siblings (or if need be, a friend and his or her siblings). It will help you develop social skills that will serve you well throughout your life.

**Your Mother**

When I was an early teen, too young to drive but old enough to have a job and earn a little bit of money, I wanted to do something special for my mom for her birthday. I decided to take her to a dinner theater for dinner and a play.

Bob Denver, the actor who played "Gilligan" in the TV sitcom Gilligan's Island, was going to be in town doing a show at the Gaslight Dinner Theater. I had saved up enough money to afford two tickets to the show, so I went downtown and got them. I think mom had to drive me there, so my gift to her wasn't a surprise.

I had never been to a dinner theater before. When the evening came, Mom and I drove to the theater, went in, and were seated at a table with another couple. We ordered our meals, which were served, and then we began eating. While we were having dinner, I noticed the man at our table give the waiter a small wad of cash. I leaned over to Mom and said, "I don't have any money to give the waiter," worried that I was unprepared for the social setting I was then in.

Mom assured me that I didn't need extra money. Apparently, that wasn't a tip but money for an adult beverage that we wouldn't be having anyway.

Eventually, the theater lights dimmed, the curtain opened, and we watched the play while finishing our dinner. I hope my mother had a good time that evening. I was grateful that I could do that for her as I recognized how, over the previous fifteen years of my life, she had raised me and my siblings as a single mom.

You don't have to take your mother to a dinner theater but look for something special you can do with her. Have a night out with your mom where you cover the costs. Buy her some flowers for no reason. If you have moved away, call her during the week and see how she is doing. Take her on a date. Ask her to go on a walk with you. Whatever you choose to do, she will always remember that moment.

> Quality time and expressing appreciation come in many packages. Do something kind for your mom.

## Family Outings and Vacations

When I was younger, my mother's family planned and held the first "Anderson Family Reunion." It was held at Old Faithful in Yellowstone National Park. I can barely remember staying in cabins with my mom and my siblings, my cousins, aunts, and uncles, and the matriarch of the reunion, my maternal grandmother.

The most memorable part of the trip was the drive to the park.

My oldest brother, Larry, was old enough to drive at this point. Mom sat in the middle of the back seat of our family station wagon, right beside another brother, who was just a little older than me and susceptible to motion sickness.

We were driving on a winding road.

"Mom, I think I'm going to be sick," my brother said.

Mom shouted, "Larry, pull over!"

"There's nowhere to pull over here, Mom."

Out it came, all over my mother. I remember her cupping her hands, trying to catch the vomit as my brother lost the contents of his stomach. Her cupped hands did not provide sufficient capacity for the amount that came out with the result that Mom got covered in barf.

Larry finally found a place to pull over. Mom retrieved a change of clothes from her luggage and in a small stream that happened to be nearby, she rinsed her clothes, changed them, and we got back in the car.

That was my earliest recollection of a family vacation.

If you haven't had the opportunity to go on a vacation or at least an overnight outing with your family, then take the initiative to do something together.

If you don't have the funds for a family trip, why not camp out in your backyard? Make a picnic lunch and eat it at a park or by a river. Spend a whole day together without any social media or mobile phones to interrupt you. Play games, watch a family movie, eat popcorn, stay up late. Pick something from the list below for your family to do together. Be creative!

*Figure 3. Scan this to virtually join my family and me on a vacation to some national parks.*

As you work on developing relationships, complete the following actions. This will help you gain confidence in your ability to socialize and hopefully help your family become closer, too. Remember to be a friend to your family members.

## Record your experiences, thoughts, and feelings about this section here:

_____

_____

_____

_____

_____

_____

_____

_____

_____

_____

## Healthy Relationships—Milestone #6: "Socializing with Family" Actions

| Action | Date Completed | Explanation | Examples/ Options |
|---|---|---|---|
| Visit or do something with a cousin or other relative | | Pick a cousin, aunt, uncle, or other relative outside of your immediate family and go on an outing or do something together. | • Go to a movie<br>• Play basketball, catch, pickleball, football, etc.<br>• Play a board game<br>• Go fishing<br>• Go to a sporting event |
| Enjoy a fun activity with a sibling that YOU initiate | | If you have a sibling, make sure you're doing something fun together once in a while. If you don't have any siblings, you can substitute a friend for this action. | • Play hide and go seek<br>• Put a puzzle together<br>• Fix dinner and watch a show |
| Take your mother on an evening out. | | Make sure your mother knows that you appreciate her. Take her out for an evening–you pick up the tab–and make sure it's something that she would enjoy, not just you. | • Go to a dinner theater<br>• Go out to a nice restaurant<br>• Take her to a concert or play |
| Plan and go on a family outing or vacation | | This should be at least one night away from home with multiple or all family members. | • Go camping<br>• Rent an Air BnB<br>• Have a family road trip<br>• Visit a national or state park |

## Milestone #7: Other Adults

As an older teenager, I worked in a transmission shop and being around the oil every day contributed to my acne problems. My mother arranged for me to go to a dermatologist for consultation and treatment. She went with me for the initial few appointments, but they

Other adults
- Practice introductions
- Learn and tell jokes
- Visit a Senior/veteran
- Learn dinner etiquette

turned into periodic sessions that required me to undergo an examination and sit under an ultraviolet light for a while. So, I began driving myself to the doctor's office for my appointments. I was running late and feeling self-conscious and nervous the first time I did this. Would I be expected to make a payment there? If so, did I have enough money with me? What if they asked me something I couldn't answer? All of this was compounded by the fact that I was going because I had an acne problem.

When I arrived at the doctor's office—a few minutes late—I went to the receptionist's desk and said, "I have an appointment with Dr. So-and-So."

"Oh, Dr. So-and-So isn't in today," she said.

My teenage emotions and self-conscious nervousness got the best of me. I said something like, "Well that's great" and then turned around and walked out. As I left the receptionist called after me saying something about, "Dr. Such-and-Such can see you."

Later, I told my mother what had happened and explained that I had been too embarrassed to go back. It was a real learning experience.

Learning to interact well with other people is a key to succeeding as an adult. Don't be too hard on yourself if you mess up occasionally; we all do. However, you will likely need to get out of your comfort zone in order to interact positively with others. Like everything else in this book, it is a skill you can learn. If you are naturally an introvert—someone who is uncomfortable in groups of people—you will need to practice how to engage with others in social settings.

Here are some activities and assignments that will help you develop your confidence and your ability to interact with other people.

## Learn How to Make Introductions

What do you do when you meet a new person?

Here are some practices that will help you do well when meeting people for the first time in any setting:

- Smile
- Make eye contact
- Say, "Hello, I'm _____."
- Hold out your hand for a handshake

The other person will likely shake your hand and say, "Hi, I'm Emily," to which you reply,

- "It's nice to meet you, Emily."

If they don't tell you what their name is, simply ask, "What's your name?" Remember, they may be feeling a little awkward as well. When they tell you, respond as above: "It's nice to meet you, Emily."

As you become comfortable introducing yourself to others, your confidence will increase.

Depending on the situation you are in, the next step is to become comfortable having a conversation with another person.

*Figure 4. Scan this to learn about making introductions.*

## Practice Conversations

As hard as it might be for you, the best way to become comfortable meeting other people is to become comfortable with yourself. But what do you do if you're the self-conscious type? My suggestion is that when you are meeting someone else, focus on them. Look for something unique about them; maybe it is something they are wearing such as a shirt or a hat with a team or business logo. These clues will give you something to talk about that will put them at ease, too.

You don't want to turn the conversation into an interrogation but see what you have in common with them. You might ask them where they're from or what school they attended, whether they like sports and, if so, which sport. Find out what their favorite team is. All of these are a means by which you can "break the ice" or start a conversation in a pleasant way.

Having a few funny or interesting stories or good jokes to share will help you start a conversation with people you may not know. When you are finished speaking, listen to what they have to say and make comments that show them you listened and heard what they said.

Practice speaking to yourself in front of a mirror. Get used to the sound of your voice. Think of what others may ask you and come up with your own answers. If you have a funny story or joke you think you may want to share, practice saying it. If you practice often enough, you will become comfortable with yourself, your voice, and your words.

Your primary goal in a conversation is to help the other person be at ease and have a pleasant and fun interaction. It's hard to do that if you're uptight. Practicing will help you.

> First impressions are lasting. Make it good by focusing on the other person.

**Spend Time at an Assisted Living Home**

One way you can practice with very little risk that will also give you a feeling of satisfaction is to find an assisted living home in your area and visit there regularly. Seniors who are limited in their ability to get around will love having a visit from you. You will quickly learn that you can have fun while you're learning the skills of interacting with others.

The facility will likely have games available that you can play with the residents in a common area. As you do so, you'll be developing the most important skill for conversations: listening.

Most of us listen with the intent to respond. That means we're not really listening, but rather we're thinking of the next thing we're going to say. If you're visiting someone who is happy and anxious to share their experiences, you don't have to even think about what you're going to say.

When that happens, practice paying attention. Let them know you're listening and do your best to be genuinely interested in what they're telling you. When you help a person feel as though they are understood, you are giving them one of the best gifts you can give anyone.

## Is There Such a Thing as Dinner Etiquette?

I was once invited to a Christmas dinner with a young lady friend of mine. The venue was an expensive, upper-class restaurant. It was the first (and only) time I have had escargot (cooked snails). One doesn't go to an upper-class restaurant dressed in jeans and a T-shirt. At least we didn't back then. Maybe things have changed now.

When you find yourself invited to a more formal dinner event, it helps to know how to conduct yourself. Practicing introductions and conversations may be all that you need to successfully navigate an environment that you might otherwise find intimidating, but here are a couple of other dinner etiquette guidelines. You may want to practice these in your home a few times, so that if and when you find yourself eating at a fancy, expensive restaurant, you won't freeze up or mess up.

1. Don't begin eating until everyone at your table has been served their food.
2. If a lady comes to sit at your table or stands to leave your table, you stand up.
3. If you sense there is a proper way to do things but aren't certain, ask someone or watch what others are doing and copy them.

In my early years of college, I asked a young lady to a dance. We went to dinner beforehand at a nicer restaurant. This restaurant served a bowl of shrimp with every meal. I liked shrimp. I had first tried them when I visited my cousins and we all went to a buffet restaurant that served butterflied, breaded, deep fried shrimp. I had tried one and discovered that the texture and the flavor were both enjoyable to me.

At the dinner with my date, the waiter put the shrimp bowl on the table, leaving me and my date to enjoy it. Knowing I liked shrimp, I picked one up, took a bite, and started chewing.

This shrimp was crunchier than what I remembered. I finished the one, set the tail on my plate and didn't have another one. My date didn't have any either.

Shortly after that, the waiter came back, looked at the shrimp bowl and asked, "You're not shrimp fans? Well, let me show you how to eat these."

He then took a shrimp from the bowl, pinched the legs underneath the shrimp, peeled the hard shell off the shrimp, and very graciously said, "This is how you eat these."

These were "peel-and-eat" shrimp. I was only familiar with peeled, butterflied, breaded, and deep-fried shrimp.

Suddenly the shrimp tasted much better. That first crunchy shrimp I ate had the shell, legs, and all!

If you're ever uncertain about dinner etiquette, don't be afraid to ask someone about the proper thing to do. You may also do an internet search on some topics such as, "How to eat at a fancy restaurant," or "What is the proper etiquette when eating out?" There will be a lot of great suggestions and tutorials for you to learn from. (This will also help in the section on dating.)

## Record your experiences, thoughts, and feelings about this section here:

_____

_____

_____

_____

_____

_____

_____

_____

_____

_____

_____

# Healthy Relationships—Milestone #7: "Socializing with Other Adults" Actions

| Action | Date Completed | Explanation | Examples/Options |
|---|---|---|---|
| Practice introductions | | Watch the video on self-introductions (QR code above). Find opportunities where you can practice introducing yourself to someone and introducing someone else to one of your friends. | • School or a school sporting or social event<br>• At work, meeting a new coworker or customer |
| Practice conversations | | Become comfortable speaking with other people. Generally, that means learning to listen with genuine interest, but also being prepared with something appropriate to say. School, social events, and your workplace all provide opportunities to practice conversations. In some of those places, conversations are necessary. You might as well get good at it. | • Notice unique things about the other person<br>• Use their name appropriately while speaking<br>• Make eye contact with a positive expression on your face<br>• Learn some jokes to help facilitate a conversation |
| Visit an assisted living center or an elderly neighbor | | When you visit an assisted living center or find an elderly neighbor living by themselves, you will have opportunities to practice being a good listener, making introductions, and learning how to participate in a conversation. | • Assisted living centers in your area<br>• An elderly single neighbor<br>• An elderly relative |
| Learn and practice dinner etiquette | | Practice dinner etiquette at home, so it won't be strange or awkward if and when you find yourself in a more formal dinner setting. Use the guidelines above as a starting point. | • Practice at home<br>• Practice on a date<br>• Attend formal events like a school dance or work holiday event |

## Milestone #8: Dating

Puberty can be awkward. Your body is changing physically and chemically and, in a way, it's hard to keep up with these changes.

When I was a young teenager, I went with a youth group to a roller-skating rink. Every so often the

Dating
○ Learn to dance
○ Dating etiquette
○ Go on a group date
○ Go on a date

normal lights would turn down, some colored lights would come on, and the announcer would say, "This next song is for couples only."

If you wanted to skate with a girl, you would go ask her. If she said yes, then the two of you would skate around the rink holding hands for as long as the song played. Even back then it wasn't unusual for a girl to ask a guy to skate.

One day a young lady in the group approached me and asked me to skate for one of the "couples only" songs.

I said, "No."

I don't think I even said, "No, thank you."

Looking back now, I wish I could go back and do it differently. I would accept her invitation, skate kindly with her, even hold her hand, and then thank her when we were done. Even if I wasn't attracted to her or didn't care for her, it would have been a much kinder response.

Later in high school, I had the chance to get it right.

By this time, I was old enough to drive and go on a date. There was a girl who was relatively new to the school. She wasn't unattractive, but she was a little different. She was very outgoing, and said she wanted to be a singer. She managed to get a singing gig in one of our school assemblies. Rather than singing by herself, she arranged something like a karaoke sing-along with a popular song from back in the day. It wasn't normal karaoke, though, because the vocals from the recording were playing with the music as she sang with it. What's more, it was a male vocalist on the recording.

Most of us thought it was a little different, even weird.

Guess what? She took a liking to me.

She asked me out, and we went on a couple of dates. I really wasn't attracted to her, and I don't think I misled her to think that I was, but she apparently felt like there was more of a mutual attraction.

When I look back on that now, I'm grateful that I was more gracious in my interactions with her than I had been at the skating rink. Eventually, she picked up on the fact that I was happy to be a friend but not really anything beyond that.

Back then, I usually found that when I was interested in a particular girl, she wouldn't be interested in me.

When I was a little bit older, in my early twenties, I met a girl in one of my college classes. I was definitely interested. One week I missed the class, and the next time I was there, she gave me the handouts from the previous class that I had missed, without me asking her to get them. I took that as a sign that: a) she had noticed that I wasn't there and b) she might have some interest in me.

I thanked her for doing that, and eventually asked her out.

After we had gone out a few times, I had the desire to be more serious in our relationship. When I got the courage to express those feelings to her, she kindly told me that she really didn't want to be more serious than we already were.

It hurt.

I tried to hide the hurt for the rest of that date, but I wasn't very good at faking my feelings. Something like that is probably going to happen to you. While it is difficult at the time, it isn't the end of the world. Be gracious even in your disappointment and honor her choices.

*Figure 5. Scan this to hear stepdad share some dating experiences and advice.*

## Pushing Past Your Fears

I share these stories with you because part of your success as an adult man will be your ability to have not only good friendships with young ladies but, eventually, serious relationships that can ultimately lead to marriage.

It's important for you to push past your initial fears and learn how to have positive relationships with young ladies. You are going to make some mistakes along the path. That's okay. Learn from those mistakes and keep going!

Given the prevalence of online communication options, today you have opportunities to initiate conversations without being present with the person. That might be a safer way to begin a dialogue, but don't let your online world keep you from developing the ability to comfortably have friends and girlfriends in the real world.

If you have opportunities to participate in school dances, take them. Even if you don't want to.

During one high school dance, I got up the nerve to ask an attractive girl out on a date. She was on the school drill team. We knew each other but were not close friends.

In an attempt at creativity, which wasn't uncommon back then, a person would ask a girl out with some creative event or activity. In this case, I baked a cake. In frosting on top of the cake, I asked her to go to the dance with me. I went to her home, knocked on the door, and when she answered, I gave her the cake, not expecting an immediate answer. As I was walking back to my car, she called out to me saying that she would go with me to the dance.

I was happy about that. She formalized her response with a creative reply to me a few days later. I subsequently learned that she was eager to go with me to the dance because she had already been asked by someone that she didn't want to go with, and I was her way out. I still take that as a win, even if I was the lesser of two evils: at least I wasn't the greater of two evils!

I realize that the world you are living in today is not the same as the one in which I grew up. But here's what hasn't changed: for you to become a successful adult you're going to have to learn in-person social skills and abilities, including how to ask a girl on a date, and how to navigate the sometimes tricky and sometimes painful path of relationships with the opposite sex.

What opportunities do you have to develop relationships with girls? School is likely the most common opportunity, followed by work, and other community events or gatherings. Find opportunities where you can get to know young ladies, develop friendships with them, and eventually ask them out.

## A word about gender and same-sex attraction (SSA)

Things are dramatically different in the world at the time I write this book compared to when I was growing up. What currently occupies thoughtful dialogue would never have been heard of a few decades ago, except on the fringes of society and then the conversation would have been met with great skepticism and criticism. If you are struggling with thoughts and feelings of gender confusion or same-sex attraction, or both, please know that I empathize with your difficulties.

If you feel you have dominant female traits, despite your male birth gender, I would be very cautious about thinking that you were born into the wrong gender. Having been raised in a primarily matriarchal environment, I inherited many traits from my mother, my grandmother, and the other women in my life that might have caused me to question my own gender identity if I were growing up today. Similarly, I grew up with some young ladies who were more athletic than their peers and exhibited some traits and behaviors that were more traditionally male. Back then, such a young lady would be referred to as a "tomboy." Despite having non-traditional mannerisms, traits, or characteristics, we matured into the successful people we have become, even though we possessed some characteristics considered more dominant in the opposite birth gender. In the meantime, just because you sense that you have feminine characteristics does not mean you are not a man. Those characteristics can be valuable to you as a man by helping you be better equipped emotionally to relate to a broader range of people and even more capable of loving and connecting more deeply with others.

If you have feelings of gender confusion, I suggest much caution about assuming that you are the "wrong" gender and recommend you wait until you are sufficiently mature before making any potentially permanent physical changes.

I have chosen to write this book from the perspective of a heterosexual audience primarily because that is my experience. But please know that I am sympathetic to your situation whether your experience is like mine or not. If you are physically attracted to other males, I understand that those feelings are very real, even if you may not want that to be the case. As I have not experienced this personally, I am not in a position to offer advice. But I invite you to look for other supportive people who understand how to navigate the nuances of same-sex attraction in a way that brings integrity and compassion to all your exchanges.

Your dating life is important, and it is a helpful way to develop and apply the principles that will help you be better prepared for life and all the social interactions that come with it.

Developing positive relationships with your family, friends, and the opposite sex are all steps on the path to manhood.

Here are some actions that will help you develop these skills.

## Record your experiences, thoughts, and feelings about this section here:

_____

_____

_____

_____

_____

_____

_____

_____

_____

_____

_____

# Healthy Relationships—Milestone #8: "Dating" Actions

| Action | Date Completed | Explanation | Examples/ Options |
|---|---|---|---|
| Learn how to dance, or at least learn a few dance moves | | You may or may not end up going dancing, but it is good to be prepared. With the anonymity of the internet, from the comfort of your own home, you can practice some dance moves. (It did wonders for Napoleon Dynamite.) | • Watch Michael Jackson videos (but don't expect to be that good at first)<br>• There's nothing wrong with learning ballroom dancing |
| Learn and practice dating etiquette | | Here are some of the basics. In addition to these bullet points, make sure you are genuine. When we date, we always try to be our best selves, and that is good, but make sure you are being honest in your behavior while you put your best foot forward. (Don't step on hers when you do.) | • Be on time<br>• Be polite<br>• Don't be overly physical – look for cues from your date<br>• Ask questions<br>• If you asked her out, you pay<br>• Look nice |
| Go on a group date | | It's often safer emotionally and otherwise to go on a group date first. With a friend or a few friends, plan and go on a group date together. | • Restaurant hop<br>• Pretend to be tourists<br>• Picnic<br>• Hike<br>• Play a board game |
| Go on a date | | You can't practice dating etiquette if you don't go on a date.<br><br>Remember, you date so that you can get to know someone better.<br><br>Always focus on the long term. Look for someone who could be a lifelong partner and the mother of your children. | • Go to a zoo or aquarium<br>• Build a campfire<br>• Go to dinner<br>• Fix dinner at home<br>• Go for a walk in the park & get ice cream |

# LOVE

LOVE CAN BE LEARNED

**Pets**
○ Watch a pet movie
○ Get a pet
○ Care for your pet
○ Love your pet

**Friends**
○ Give a gift
○ Send a positive note
○ Act of kindness
○ Practice empathy

**Family**
○ Help a sibling
○ Read a story to a child
○ Letter to grandparents
○ Note to your mother

**You**
○ List what you like
○ Letter to your younger self
○ Write your life's lessons
○ A letter to your dad

# Path #3:
# Learn to Love;
# The Most Important Path
# on the Journey to Manhood

When was the time that you felt the most loved in your childhood? Think back to the circumstances of that time. Who did that love for you come from?

When was the time that you felt the most love for someone else? Who was that person?

Your answers to those questions may not be the same as mine, but for me, it was my mother. As the youngest of five children in a single parent household, I was probably a bit spoiled. And if feeling the unconditional love of a mother makes one spoiled, then I certainly was.

As an adult looking back, I can see how easy it would have been for my mother to be disappointed, frustrated, or even resentful about the fact that as her marriage was falling apart, she found herself pregnant with her fifth child. She was going to have to take care of that baby without her husband's help.

Rather than be resentful, however, my mother found some solace in parenting her new little boy. And I felt her love from my earliest memories. She would read stories to me at bedtime. If I fell asleep in her bed, often

I would awake in the morning by her side. At church if I were sleepy, she would run her fingers through my hair as I laid on the pew with my head in her lap. Even as a teenager, and the last child in the house, mom would do things with me that most mothers wouldn't. We would go on overnight campouts together and try to find where the fish were biting. I have many fond memories of my mother's love.

You may not think love has much to do with becoming a man, but it has everything to do with it. You cannot be a successful man without learning how to love others, and you cannot fully love others until you learn to love yourself. Learning to love yourself may be the toughest milestone on the journey to manhood that you face. Despite my mother's love, lacking the presence and love of my father caused me to doubt myself. Learning to love has been one of the biggest challenges of overcoming my fatherlessness.

The good news is that you can learn to love yourself and others. Like learning to play a particular sport or develop a specific talent, it takes effort, practice, and persistence, but you can come to love yourself. Until you do, you will be limited in your ability to love others.

We'll start with practicing to love your pets.

> Self-love isn't just a catch phrase. Learning to love oneself allows you to love others.

## Milestone #9: Love Your Pets

When we were growing up, we had cats. The female cats were not always spayed, (we called them "fixed"), so several of our cats had kittens. It was exciting for me to watch the momma cat raise her kittens from the time they were born (which my older siblings seemed to oversee), until the kittens were old enough to be adopted out. I remember putting a  hand-written cardboard sign on the tree in front of our house that said, "Free Kittens." It didn't take long until they all found good homes.

When I was a young teenager, one of our cats had a batch of kittens and all but one was adopted. Mom didn't want to have more cats in the house than we already had, so after the "Free Kittens" sign didn't work for this last kitten, we asked the humane society to find a home for him. This little kitten had been with us about six to eight weeks, and I had become quite attached to it. I went with Mom to the animal shelter, but I was so sad when I got home without the kitten that I cried. I worried because I understood the policy at the time was that if the kitten wasn't adopted within two weeks, the shelter would put it "to sleep."

It broke my heart to think of euthanizing that little kitten. My mother must have had a hard time seeing me so sad about that possibility because she took me back within a day or two to retrieve the kitten. When we got there, it was gone.

Knowing the kitten was gone made me feel better. I loved the kitten, but my concern was that the kitten would be deprived of life if no one adopted him. Since it wasn't there after only a day or two, I understood that it had been safely adopted.

I hope you have the opportunity to have pets when you're growing up. I'm most fond of cats, but we also had dogs.

As my wife and I have been raising our own children, we've had cats, mice, (sometimes at the same time, and in one instance, that didn't end well for the mouse), hamsters, fish, birds, and even a hermit crab. Some pets have been cuddlier than others, but when you have a pet, you learn responsibility and you learn to love. Having a pet will give you the chance to practice love. For some, it might be the starting point to developing this emotion.

One day my brother and I were coming home from a friend's house. We were across the street from our home when one of our siblings opened the front door and called something out to us. At the time, my brother had a pet dog. He was something of a dachshund mix. I referred to him as a wiener dog. He managed to get out the door and then came running across the street toward us. To our horror, at the same time a car came down the street and accidentally hit our pet dog. I remember seeing him roll under the tires of the car. We were shocked when he got to his feet and ran, yelping, back to our house.

Because he was still moving, I was hopeful that he would be okay. Mom wrapped the dog in a blanket, and we gathered quietly around him. Gradually his movements slowed down and he died a few minutes after being hit.

It was heartbreaking.

If you have your heart broken by the loss of a pet, then you know you have the ability to love.

Practice loving your pets, so that you can develop your ability to love.

Use the table below to track your completion of the items on this milestone. The "Explanation" and "Examples/Options" columns give suggestions for each requirement.

## Learn to Love—Milestone #9: "Love Your Pets" Actions

| Action | Date Completed | Explanation | Examples/ Options |
|---|---|---|---|
| Watch a non-animated movie about a pet | | If you don't already have a pet of your own, you can have a vicarious experience from watching a movie. As a young boy I watched the movie, Old Yeller and I still remember the emotions I felt about that dog. | • Old Yeller (1957 Disney)<br>• Lassie<br>• Beethoven |
| Get a pet | | If you are a minor, this will require the approval of your mother or guardian. I suggest a cat or a dog. I tend to prefer cats but have had both. Fish don't count for this action. You need to be able to cuddle this pet. | • Cat<br>• Dog<br>• An animal that will respond positively when you hug it |
| Care for your pet for at least 6 months | Start:<br>_____<br>Complete:<br>_____ | Caring for your pet primarily involves two tasks: feeding and cleaning up after it. If you have a dog, a daily walk or play time is also needful. | • Feed<br>• Clean up after it (Scoop the poop from the yard or cat box) regularly and consistently<br>• Walk the dog |
| Show love for your pet | | The whole point of this group of actions is to increase your ability to love. Practice loving your pet by showing it love. See if you feel love and affection from your pet. (That's why some pets are better than others for this action group.) | • Hug your pet<br>• Speak kindly to your pet<br>• Express love to your pet |

## Record your experiences, thoughts, and feelings about this section here:

_____

_____

_____

_____

_____

_____

_____

_____

_____

_____

## Milestone #10: Love Your Friends

I know we just talked about having friends, being good friends and choosing your friends carefully. Our focus in that section was on developing positive relationships, which is important.

For this milestone on the Map to Manhood we're going to focus on a particular component of your friendships: learning to love your friends.

Every week in the summer, my friend Danny and I would mow a widowed neighbor lady's lawn. We would split the proceeds, take the bus downtown, and go to the model shop. We would each buy a plastic model airplane, come home, and then spend the afternoon putting the airplanes together and painting them.

Danny was a little older than me, but we did a lot of other things together. We watched Saturday morning cartoons, played driveway basketball, and we even made a movie together with Danny's older brother and younger sister. It was called, "A Jungle Battle" (Scan the QR code to watch it if you like.)

*Figure 6. Scan this to watch "A Jungle Battle"*

We had a lot of fun together. But Danny wasn't my only childhood friend.

At some point in my childhood, my mom had a garage built at the end of our driveway. My older brothers constructed a basketball backboard and hoop and mounted it to the gable of the garage. In the 1970s, our video game options were non-existent. ("Pong," the first commercially successful video game, came out in 1972, but it took a while for it to catch on.) Consequently, we spent a lot of time playing basketball in our driveway. In the winter we would shovel the snow off the driveway and then play. We even had a floodlight mounted to our house that illuminated the court so we could play at night. We had a lot of fun playing basketball together.

After playing basketball with some of my friends, Larry and Eric in particular, we would take turns buying each other Slurpees. (Usually not in the winter, though.) One time it was my turn, but I didn't have the money. I went inside and told mom, and she gladly gave me the $3 to buy the Slurpees.

You are growing up in a day when you have more opportunity to interact with people online or electronically than you do in person. The problem with this is that you don't learn how to interact as a human with another human. And you don't get to share Slurpees with your friends! Most of the meaningful communication in your life will be in person, not online. You will want to hang out in person with your friends regularly, so find good things to do with them. Maybe you can play basketball together and then go get Slurpees. As you spend time together, you will be developing your abilities in ways you don't even realize, but most importantly, you'll be developing your ability to love your friends.

When I was growing up, it wasn't cool to even think about loving your friends, let alone talk about it. But love was the bond that defined our friendship. We knew it, though it was unspoken. You don't have to tell your friends that you love them, but it's okay, and even good for you, to realize that it is love that is the bond and basis of your friendship. And that's a good thing because it's helping you develop the ability to love.

In the table below there are four actions that you can take that will help deepen the bonds of love in your friendships.

**Record your experiences, thoughts, and feelings about this section here. Pay particular attention to your ability to love others:**

_____

_____

_____

_____

_____

_____

# Learn to Love—Milestone #10: "Love Your Friends" Actions

| Action | Date Completed | Explanation | Examples/ Options |
|---|---|---|---|
| Give a gift to a (non-girl) friend | | It doesn't have to be expensive or elaborate but give a present to one of your friends. A birthday present is okay, but giving a gift for no special reason is better. Put some thought into it. | • A copy of a favorite movie<br>• A gift card to a favorite store<br>• A nice article of clothing |
| Send a positive note or message to a friend daily four times in one week | | Hopefully you have at least four friends or acquaintances. (If not, work on Path #2, Milestone #1.)<br><br>Send a note, text, or voice message to a different friend at least four times in one week. | • Text, "I had fun yesterday. So glad we're friends"<br>• Mail a "Thank you" card or a generic card or note<br>• Send an email saying, "I'm glad we're friends" |
| Do an act of service | | Look for an opportunity to do something for one of your friends that would help them, and that they would appreciate (as in the example of Lynn loaning me his car at the last minute). | • Help with homework<br>• Help with housework or yardwork |
| Practice empathy | | Empathy is the ability to put yourself in someone else's position and feel and understand what they may be going through. It helps to be a good friend if you can empathize with them. When you notice one of your friends having a hard time, try to put yourself in their situation and see how you would feel. Be genuine. | • When successful, statements like, "That must feel awful" or "I understand how you're feeling" express empathy |

## Milestone #11: Love Your Family

What is the difference between socializing with your family, which we discussed previously, and loving your family?

Let's take a look.

I am the youngest of five kids. My next oldest brother is a year-and-a-half older than me. We didn't always get along.

Once, when I was fifteen, I needed or wanted to go somewhere. My older brother had a car. He overheard what I said, rolled over in the recliner where he was half asleep, dropped his car keys on the floor and said, "You can take my car."

Holy Cow! We spent more time arguing during our teenage years than helping each other. I didn't expect such a generous offer.

I couldn't even legally drive, though I knew how. I couldn't get my license until I was sixteen, and I didn't yet have a learner's permit.

But I was never one to pass up a good opportunity.

I thanked him, picked up his keys and took his car before he could change his mind! I ended up with a friend of mine cruising our neighborhood. I remember getting nervous going onto Tenth North Street, because the speed limit was 35 miles per hour.

Fortunately, we made it home safely, with no accidents or tickets, and I returned my brother's keys and car to him.

When you have opportunities to help your siblings, help them. Do it with as much genuine love and selflessness as you can muster. You'll be amazed at how it will improve your relationships at home.

You don't have to lend them your car (especially if they're not old enough to legally drive) but pay attention and you will find something that is within your ability to do. Then do it.

When I was in grade school, my bedtime was earlier than my older siblings'. It was frustrating to me that I had to go to bed while they were still up watching TV or talking or doing something else. One time, I remember my older brother Scott coming into my room when I was supposed to go to bed, and he offered to read to me since I had to go to bed earlier.

I had a book from the library that I was interested in, so he sat down next to my bed and started reading.

I was interested in the story, and he kept reading. After a while he said, "Doesn't this book have any chapters?" Apparently, it didn't. He had planned to read until the chapter ended, but this book wasn't divided into chapters. Five decades later, I still remember how nice it was that my older brother read to me while I was supposed to be going to sleep. If you have any younger siblings, perhaps you could do the same thing for them.

## When Siblings Fight

Since Mom was gone most of the day, my siblings and I were pretty much on our own. When we got into arguments, which happened frequently, there was no responsible adult to step in and calm things down. As the yelling escalated, it would usually end with me yelling a few choice phrases like, "I HATE YOU!" after which I would run into my room and slam the door. (This only partially helped because I shared the same bedroom with the sibling with whom I was arguing.)

The slammed door was sometimes followed by a kick from the outside. More than one bedroom door in our house had been patched after holes had been kicked in them. If you have ever felt like this, you may feel like loving your family is nearly impossible. Loving your family may be more difficult than loving your pets or your friends, but with practice, you can do it.

Deep down in your heart, you already do.

My grandma would often come and stay at our home. She lived in a small farming community about two-and-a-half hours from our suburban city home. Grandma would play games with me when I was younger and bake bread and sew while she was with us. I'm sure she came to help Mom care for us kids—and particularly me, since I was the youngest—but Grandma was a critical woman. She was a farmer's wife and valued work. In her opinion, if you didn't work hard, you weren't worth much.

As kids, we didn't like to work. Often, Grandma would complain about how lazy we were. Her criticism was not always welcome. I frankly didn't like it. My siblings didn't care for it, either. I assumed my mom wanted us to work harder and be more responsible, but she advocated for us kids against her mother's criticism.

One day my mom apparently had had enough. I don't remember what was said, but I do remember uneasily witnessing the argument between my mom and her mom, my grandmother. While they were arguing, I felt defensive of my mom, and I shared her anger and frustration over my grandmother's persistent criticism.

Grandma finally said something like, "Well, if I'm not appreciated, I'll just go and not come back." She gathered her things, got in her car, and went home. When Grandma left, something I didn't expect happened to my feelings. As soon as she walked out the door, I started to cry. I turned to my mom and said, "What if she never comes back?" As the argument culminated in Grandma leaving, my biggest fear was that she would never come back. (She did.)

Even though you may feel anger and even hatred towards your siblings, perhaps even your mom, and very likely your dad, deep in your heart there is an even stronger feeling of love.

That love is important. It is the key to your future manhood.

## The Upside of Negative Emotions

When you feel what you would describe as hate, realize that you wouldn't feel that way if you didn't already have feelings of love for that person. Hate isn't the opposite of love. Hate is, at minimum, evidence of a desire to love, if not evidence that love already exists. If you feel hatred, it may be because the love you feel is not being reciprocated as you want or expect.

Indifference is the opposite of love. Truly not caring about someone—whether they are happy or hurt, in pain or healthy, alive or dead—is the opposite of love.

Learning to develop your ability to love is the single most important skill that will help you grow into manhood.

Being a man is not about being harsh, critical, unfeeling, or rude.

Just the opposite is true.

Being able to refrain from responding rudely or with anger when others treat you rudely or meanly is an indication of maturity beyond what most adults acquire. That doesn't mean it's easy, but you can do it. Practice by learning to love your family members.

> *Your ability to love is the single most important skill to develop.*

Every once in a while, you can say something nice to your family members. Every week, perhaps every day, you can do some act of service for your mom or one of your brothers or sisters, or a grandparent. Remember the vacation story about our family reunion in Yellowstone? Don't forget all the times that your mother has been there taking care of you, maybe even cupping her hands trying to catch your vomit when you were sick. Take a minute and think about everything your mother has done for you, and then thank her.

Practice loving your family and showing that love through little acts of kindness and positive comments.

## Record your experiences, thoughts, and feelings about this section here.

_____

_____

_____

_____

_____

_____

_____

_____

_____

## Learn to Love—Milestone #11: "Love Your Family" Actions

| Action | Date Completed | Explanation | Examples/ Options |
|---|---|---|---|
| Help one of your siblings with something important to them. | | Step back from worrying or thinking about yourself and try to see things through the eyes of one of your siblings. As you do, ask yourself, "what does he/she want or need that I could help with?" | • Help with homework<br>• Help with housework<br>• Get them a thoughtful gift |
| Read a bedtime story to a younger sibling | | If you don't have a younger sibling, find some equivalent way to serve someone younger than you. Perhaps a cousin or a friend's sibling. | • The Levan Thumps series<br>• The Michael Vey series<br>• The Fable Haven series<br>• *The Chronicles of Narnia*<br>• *The Boxcar Children*<br>• The Nancy Drew series<br>• The Hardy Boys series |
| Write a letter to your grandparent(s) | | Write a list of things you appreciate about your grandparent(s) and then send it to them in a letter, in an envelope with a stamp... "snail mail." | • Consider fun times you've had with them<br>• What lessons have you learned from them?<br>• What about them do you admire? |
| Write a note/ letter to your mother | | You could leave a note somewhere your mother will discover it when you're not around. Think of all that your mother has done for you and tell her what she means to you. | • Write it on her bathroom mirror in dry erase marker<br>• Hide a note under her pillow or in her purse<br>• Send it in the mail |

## Milestone #12: Love Yourself

On your entire journey to manhood, this is the most important milestone. If you want to be able to love others, you have to learn to love yourself.

Growing up, I liked kids. I looked forward to the time when I would have kids of my own. Sometimes, however, I did get frustrated with them. I remember babysitting one of my nieces when I was an older teenager and, for whatever reason, she cried a lot that evening. It didn't take long for a screaming upset baby to burn through whatever patience and control I had as a teenager. After about thirty minutes of doing everything I could think of to calm her down, I held her on my shoulder, patted her back, and screamed along with her out of my own frustration.

Despite that experience, I still loved kids. And the question I never realized I had until later in life was, "how could my dad have ever left me?" It made no sense to me, especially as I knew, without a doubt, that I wanted to have children of my own. On some level, I painfully concluded that there must have been something wrong with me; I wasn't important enough for him to stay. Why else would he leave? These were the thoughts I had as a little boy, not knowing any of the details of my parents' divorce.

Eventually, I came to understand that Dad didn't leave "me." My parents divorced after their marriage fell apart. Logically, I understood that Dad left Mom, not me. Despite understanding this logically, my feelings of not measuring up persisted and continued to negatively impact many important areas of my life. The feelings, ideas, and beliefs we develop as we are growing up are often difficult to change. Even when you begin to understand why your dad has not been in your life, your feelings about that abandonment don't necessarily change.

I tell you this because you may have those same ideas in your mind and those feelings in your heart. You might wonder if there is something wrong with you or feel that you weren't important enough to your dad.

If you are going to learn how to love others, you need to love yourself, too, but it's hard to love yourself if you feel like there is something wrong with you. Sometimes bad things happen to innocent people. It doesn't mean they did something wrong. Please hear these words and know I am speaking directly to you: the fact that your dad left your family doesn't mean there is something wrong with you. And if you have been feeling like something might be wrong with you because your dad left, this next section is the most important part of this whole book. Unless you work through this emotionally, it is likely to be the biggest hurdle to your future success in any area of your life.

## How to Heal So You Can Love Yourself

My siblings and I visited Dad regularly while we were growing up. I have fond memories of visiting him and my stepmom, who were both good to us. At that time, Dad was an owner in an apparently successful business. He had a nice home overlooking the ocean. He drove nice cars.

When we visited, he would take us to amusement parks and museums in southern California. We went deep sea fishing on his boat. I was afraid of getting seasick and throwing up but, fortunately, I kept the contents of my stomach inside. (My brother wasn't so lucky.)

Every Christmas he would give each of us a gift certificate for $25 to JC Penney's. That was like $100 or more back then. To a little kid, it felt like I had won the lottery! When I was with Dad, I didn't feel that he didn't like me. What I didn't realize was that I had subconsciously concluded that he didn't love me. On that level, I rationalized that if he loved me, he would have figured out how to make things work with my mom. He would have figured out how to keep our family together because of that love. Since he didn't do that, my conclusion was that he must not have loved me.

What was wrong with me? I tried to understand.

I knew Mom loved me. Mom was my world, especially as a little boy. She was there for me. She was the one taking care of all five of her children.

When I was too sick to go to school and Mom had to go to work, she would have to find a neighbor who could take care of me during her workday. An older couple that lived two doors down would take me in for the day. Their house was dark. It smelled of cigarette smoke. They were quiet and kept to themselves. They were very nice, but it was not a place where a little boy wanted to go to spend a whole day. I didn't look forward to Mom leaving when I had to go to their house. I wanted to stay with Mom. I really wanted Mom to stay home with me and not go to work. I thought that if Dad really loved me, he would have stayed with my mom, not gotten a divorce, and when I got sick, my mom could then be home to care for me.

The hardest thing about the thought of being unloved and abandoned by my dad, was that it was subconscious, which means I didn't know I had it.

I was doing well in school.

I had friends.

I had fun with my family, in between the arguments. I had extended family members that we occasionally visited. I had fun with them.

I didn't think there was anything wrong with me consciously.

But in my subconscious mind was this constant, dark thought spreading to my heart that there must be something wrong with me. It was the only thing that made sense, because why else would my dad choose to leave me?

And all these thoughts were happening without me being aware of them.

If you are growing up or have grown up without your dad, and you think you might have some thoughts and feelings like that, then pay attention to this next part. Your dad's absence from your daily life doesn't mean something is wrong with you. And you can understand in your conscious mind. But if your subconscious mind doesn't agree, it will win every time.

> *It isn't your fault. Just because someone isn't in your life doesn't mean something is wrong with you.*

So how do you get your subconscious mind to consider a different possibility? Here are some things you can do to help learn to love yourself:

- **Start a list of what you like about yourself.**

  From the time you were young right up until today, you have said or done things that you liked. Do you like your hair? Your sense of humor? How you help other people feel good? Often, we tend to remember the things we don't like, or that we did wrong. Start now listing and reviewing the things you do like about yourself. Keep a short version of it with you. When you're feeling down about yourself, pull out your list and read it. If you can, read it out loud. It may seem silly to you, but it will help you recognize that there are many good things about you.

**Things I like about me:**

_____   _____

_____   _____

_____   _____

- **Write a letter to your younger self**

  Whatever age you are now, from fourteen to forty, you know more about life than you did when you were little. Do you think you understand some things that your four-year-old self didn't know or understand? Writing about the experiences you've had—and the wisdom you've gained from life—can help heal the emotional wounds that your "younger self" may still carry.

  Think about yourself when you were younger. Visualize your current or future, more mature self, sitting down with your four-year-old self. Write a letter to that little boy about all the things you have learned, how you have grown, and how you have learned to love who you are. Imagine that little boy sitting across from you and have a conversation with him. Tell your four-year-old self how much you love him. Tell him what things he has to look forward to in life. Give him the advice that you know he needs to go through life successfully. Use the space provided below, or write it in your journal.

**Dear Four-Year-Old Me:**          **Date:** _____

_____

_____

_____

_____

_____

_____

_____

_____

_____

_____

_____

_____

_____

_____

_____

_____

_____

_____

_____

_____

_____

_____

_____

_____

- **Extracting the Lessons from Your Life**

At Christmas time, my mom would often bring home a bunch of mixed nuts in their shells. I learned to like eating nuts. Pecans, walnuts, peanuts, almonds, Brazil nuts, chestnuts, etc. I found that I enjoyed eating them all. I had to use a nutcracker—it was like a pair of pliers—to crack the hard shell around the outside so I could get at the nut inside.

It took some effort.

Every nut I wanted to eat had a shell around it that I had to crack open. The lessons that your subconscious mind wants to learn from your experiences are like the nuts inside shells. In order to get them, you have to crack the shell and open it up.

This exercise is like cracking the shell around some of the bad, scary, or even traumatic experiences you may have had up to this point in your life. You may feel like you've tried to crack some of these nuts open and the shells were very hard. Sometimes it seems easier to leave the nut alone and go find something else to eat. The problem is that the nut doesn't go away. It keeps getting in your way until you crack it open, learn the lesson from it, and feel genuine gratitude that you had the opportunity to "eat" that nut.

Here is how this process works.

Think about a time when you felt angry, then write about it on the pages below. It may help to start with your earliest memory of the emotion. Answer the questions for that instance and then think of the next memory of the emotion and do it again. If you prefer, or if you need additional space, use a notepad or journal.

Ask yourself, "What caused me to feel angry? Then write the answer on the paper. Write down everything you can think of that led up to you feeling angry.

Then write the question, "What lessons have I learned from this experience?"

Write down all the lessons that you have learned from that experience. For instance, did you learn to be more patient with yourself? Did you learn that you needed attention and didn't get it? Did you learn that others around you might have had difficulties with the problems they themselves were dealing with?

Once you have written down all the lessons you can think of, write, "What else can I learn from this experience?" and write down all the other thoughts and ideas that come to your mind.

After you have written down everything you can think of, read the list a few times. Keep that list with you. When you feel angry, review the lessons you learned from feeling angry previously.

When you do this, you are helping your subconscious mind to let go of the emotions, while keeping all the learning that can come from the experience.

When you go through this writing exercise, you will begin to feel a calmness inside. Your subconscious mind will feel much more comfortable knowing it has learned what it needed to learn from the negative experience.

You can even let go of your anger towards your dad, as you learn the lessons that you have had the opportunity to learn because he wasn't there or isn't there.

Do this exercise not only for your feelings of anger but also for hurt, sadness, guilt, and shame.

This will help you learn to love yourself.

Loving yourself will allow you to love others. It will help you do the most good in the world that you can. It will help you discover your purpose in life and help you accomplish that purpose.

Go through the following pages and write down the answers for each of your feelings.

## A Time When I Felt ANGER:

## Describe what happened:

_____

_____

_____

_____

_____

_____

_____

_____

## What caused me to feel angry?

_____

_____

_____

_____

_____

_____

## What lessons can I learn from this experience?

_____

_____

_____

_____

_____

_____

**What lessons does my subconscious mind need to learn from this experience?**

_____

_____

_____

_____

_____

_____

_____

**What else can I learn from this experience?**

_____

_____

_____

_____

_____

_____

_____

_____

Have your feelings changed after completing this exercise? If not, there may be additional experiences in your past where you felt this emotion. Complete the exercise for those experiences, too. (Use additional paper or your personal journal as needed.)

**A Time When I Felt HURT:**

**Describe what happened:**

_____

_____

_____

_____

_____

_____

_____

_____

**What caused me to feel angry?**

_____

_____

_____

_____

_____

_____

_____

**What lessons can I learn from this experience?**

_____

_____

_____

_____

_____

_____

_____

**What lessons does my subconscious mind need to learn from this experience?**

_____

_____

_____

_____

_____

_____

_____

**What else can I learn from this experience?**

_____

_____

_____

_____

_____

_____

_____

_____

Have your feelings changed after completing this exercise? If not, there may be additional experiences in your past where you felt this emotion. Complete the exercise for those experiences, too. (Use additional paper or your personal journal as needed.)

**A Time When I Felt SADNESS:**

**Describe what happened:**

_____

_____

_____

_____

_____

_____

_____

**What caused me to feel angry?**

_____

_____

_____

_____

_____

_____

**What lessons can I learn from this experience?**

_____

_____

_____

_____

_____

_____

**What lessons does my subconscious mind need to learn from this experience?**

_____

_____

_____

_____

_____

_____

_____

**What else can I learn from this experience?**

_____

_____

_____

_____

_____

_____

_____

_____

Have your feelings changed after completing this exercise? If not, there may be additional experiences in your past where you felt this emotion. Complete the exercise for those experiences, too. (Use additional paper or your personal journal as needed.)

**A Time When I Felt GUILT:**

**Describe what happened:**

_____

_____

_____

_____

_____

_____

_____

**What caused me to feel angry?**

_____

_____

_____

_____

_____

**What lessons can I learn from this experience?**

_____

_____

_____

_____

_____

_____

**What lessons does my subconscious mind need to learn from this experience?**

_____

_____

_____

_____

_____

_____

**What else can I learn from this experience?**

_____

_____

_____

_____

_____

_____

_____

_____

Have your feelings changed after completing this exercise? If not, there may be additional experiences in your past where you felt this emotion. Complete the exercise for those experiences, too. (Use additional paper or your personal journal as needed.)

**A Time When I Felt SHAME:**

**Describe what happened:**

_____

_____

_____

_____

_____

_____

_____

_____

**What caused me to feel angry?**

_____

_____

_____

_____

_____

_____

**What lessons can I learn from this experience?**

_____

_____

_____

_____

_____

_____

_____

**What lessons does my subconscious mind need to learn from this experience?**

_____

_____

_____

_____

_____

_____

**What else can I learn from this experience?**

_____

_____

_____

_____

_____

_____

_____

_____

Have your feelings changed after completing this exercise? If not, there may be additional experiences in your past where you felt this emotion. Complete the exercise for those experiences, too. (Use additional paper or your personal journal as needed.)

## A Letter to Your Dad

I attended a workshop once that was designed to help the participants have emotional breakthroughs. There were probably about 200 people or more in attendance. As part of the event, the facilitator invited attendees who were open to the idea to write their name on a piece of paper and put it in a bowl for a chance to come on stage to participate with her later that day. I didn't plan on doing that, but thought, "What the heck – the odds are practically zero that my name will be picked." So, I put my name on a piece of paper and dropped it in the bowl before the first morning break.

Imagine my surprise when I was the second person called to be on stage with the facilitator.

As it turned out, the "breakthrough" I had was related to my relationship with my dad. After asking numerous questions, observing, and listening to my responses, the facilitator gave me a specific assignment. She told me to pick a date and time when I would go out into the woods and have a conversation with my dad.

My dad had long since died, so this was not going to be an in-person conversation with him, but a chance for me to go out into nature, let my feelings come out and converse with Dad as though he were there. I reluctantly agreed and picked a date about a month away. When that date arrived, I drove to a secluded location, walked a distance away from my vehicle, and had a conversation with my dad.

It was difficult.

"How could you leave me?"

"How could you leave us?"

"Why did you do that!?"

"Why did you hurt us so much?"

When you have been emotionally hurt, you can't heal by thinking your way through it. You have to go through the emotions.

Once I had had my "conversation" with my dad, I could finally move past the hurt. Now I can truly say that I love my dad. I'm grateful he was my father. I learned things from him that I otherwise wouldn't have learned. Perhaps the biggest lesson was that I didn't want to do what he did.

I didn't want to pass the same hurt onto my own children or others in my life. Because I worked on healing myself, I am now able to help others who have similar challenges.

The last action of this milestone is similar to my talk-with-my-dad experience, but I'm not asking you to go into the forest and have a conversation with your dad. (If you think that will help you, by all means, do it!)

Whether you have a "conversation" with your dad or not, sit down and write a letter to him. It may help you to write out your frustrations, anger, and hurt. Share these feelings with him as if he were with you. You won't be sending this letter to him, even if he is alive, unless you think it will help both of you.

In your letter, tell your dad:

- how you feel
- what you hope for in your relationship
- how you would like things to be between you

Once you have written everything you can think of, tell him that you are grateful for him. Tell him that you are grateful for what you have learned from him. Tell him that you have forgiven him and ask him to forgive you too. If your relationship with him was not so negative that you can find a sliver of love in your heart for him, then tell him that, too. As I said, if you feel that sharing this letter with your dad would help your relationship, go ahead. If your dad has died, or if you are uncomfortable with sharing these things with him, or he's not ready to hear it, then keep the letter to yourself. But write it!

> Thinking versus feeling:
> You can't think your way
> through being hurt;
> you have to go
> through the emotions.

**Dear Dad:**                    **Date:** _____

_____

_____

_____

_____

_____

_____

_____

_____

_____

_____

_____

_____

_____

_____

_____

_____

_____

_____

_____

_____

After you have completed these exercises, you will be in a better position to love yourself. If you find loving yourself hard at times, remember that you are loved.

Love yourself.

# Learn to Love—Milestone #12: "Love Yourself" Actions

| Action | Date Completed | Explanation | Examples/ Options |
|---|---|---|---|
| List what you like about yourself | | Start with what you like about yourself. If you have a hard time, ask your friends and family what they like about you. Don't be too hard on yourself. Be honest. Add to the list as you develop and recognize other positive things about yourself. | • I'm good at school<br>• I'm a good friend<br>• I like my hair<br>• I have a good smile<br>• I learn things quickly |
| Write a letter to your four-year-old self | | You know more now than you did when you were four. You have learned lessons, some of them important and helpful. Take the time to write a note or letter to your younger self sharing your thoughts, advice, and love. | • Use the space provided above or record it in your journal |
| Extract Life's Lessons | | Go through the exercise above thinking about the earliest memories you have of feeling anger, hurt, sadness, guilt, and shame. | • Record the lessons from those experiences<br>• Review the list of lessons periodically |
| Write a letter to your dad | | It's okay to express any anger or frustration you may have toward your dad in this letter. You are not intending to send this letter to him. It is for you. Include in your letter what you are grateful for about your dad and, if you can, that you love him. | • Express feelings of anger or frustration if you have them<br>• Include positive experiences you've had<br>• If needed, write that you forgive your dad<br>• Express your gratitude and love for your dad |

## Record your experiences, thoughts, and feelings about this section here.

---

---

---

---

---

---

---

---

---

---

---

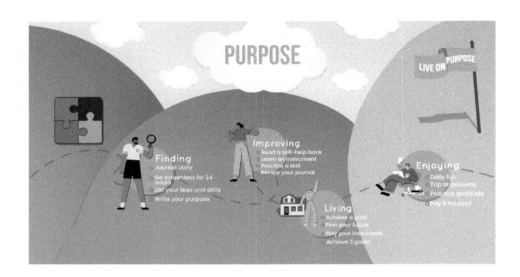

# Path #4: Discover Your Purpose – You're Here for a Reason

I've got a two-stroke, gas-powered weed-whacker. This is not a top-of-the-line weed-whacker. It usually takes some coaxing to get it to start. When it does, I have to gradually adjust the choke as it warms up. Sometimes the weed-whacker stalls when I'm trying to give it more gas before it is fully warm. But once it's running, I notice something interesting. When I am using it to edge the lawn, it spins at a certain RPM. As I move it into the grass, the torque seems to pick up. It leans into the work. It works better when it is trimming than when it is just spinning in the air. It works best when it is doing what it was designed to do. It is almost like it is happier when it is digging into its purpose.

When you know what your purpose is and you are doing it, you will have much more fulfillment and satisfaction in your life.

So, my question for you is, "What is your purpose?"

And you are the only one who can answer this question.

I used a lot of masking tape when I was a boy. I would wrap it on itself to make different shapes, then tape them together to come up with things like a crude-looking bird or an airplane. It was one of the things I could do to entertain myself, before the era of smart phones, videos, and social media.

Later, as I noticed my older siblings and friends mixing electronics into their homemade projects, I got more creative, too. I took a wooden dowel between two and three feet long, a small cardboard box, a little electric motor powered by four D-cell batteries, some string, and, of course, the ever-present masking tape, and I made a crane.

I had gotten a toggle switch from Radio Shack that you could throw one way or the other. When the motor was powered one way, the string would wind up, raising the "load" I was moving with my crane. When it was powered the other way, it would unwind or lower the load. It wasn't much to look at, but it was pretty creative.

When the mother of one of my friends saw the crane I had made, she said, "You would be good at engineering."

"Hmmm," I thought. "What is an engineer?" I thought they only drove trains.

In the sixth or seventh grade, the students at my school all took an aptitude test to help us figure out what we would like to do, and what we would be good at doing as a profession in adulthood. I remember I scored high in the potential for becoming an airline pilot.

It seems like a lot to ask someone in grade school to choose what they want to be when they grow up. We don't even know all the possibilities available to us when we're that young! How can we expect ourselves to know what we want to do as an adult? What I have since learned is that it's okay to have a direction for the present moment, knowing that, if necessary, we can change directions later. It's better to be going somewhere than to be afraid to make a decision and end up going nowhere.

**Exploring Your Options**

Growing up is a time to explore what you like, what you don't like, what you seem to be good at, and what you absolutely hate doing (besides chores!).

All of these are clues to your purpose. I'm not just talking about your career choice; I'm talking about what gives your life meaning. Once you find out what that is, you can be like the weed-whacker cutting into the grass. If you don't have a purpose—or don't know what yours is—you are like the weed-whacker when it is just spinning or when it is warming up. You don't run as well when you aren't doing what you are meant to do.

Unfortunately, someone else can't tell you what your purpose is. You must find it out for yourself. But here is a clue: there is no purpose without people. That means if you live only for yourself, you are only living half a life.

One of the few survivors of the Nazi concentration camps during World War II was a Jewish psychiatrist named Viktor Frankl. He had gone through things that you and I would have a hard time even imagining, let alone experiencing. And most of the people living in the camp with him, including his family members, died. He later wrote a book called Man's Search for Meaning. In his book, which I recommend you read, Frankl wrote, "Life asks you the meaning of life by questioning you; you don't ask life. It's not what you expect from life, but what life expects from you."

> Find your purpose
> by making the decision
> to act instead of
> going nowhere.
> Even wrong turns
> are opportunities
> for learning.

## Milestone #13: Discover Your Purpose

So how can you figure out what life expects of you? Writing in a journal—taking a short-term break from screens, social media, and other distractions—and using that opportunity to think and write about what you like and don't like, about the skills you have, will bring you closer to understanding what life expects from you. Let's look at each of these steps.

### Keep a Journal

What do Leonardo da Vinci, Thomas Edison, Albert Einstein, Oprah Winfrey, Lady Gaga, and Ronald Reagan all have in common?

They all keep (or kept) a journal.

Every day you experience thoughts and feelings. Frustration with family. Fun with friends. Disappointment that things didn't happen the way you wanted them to. Taking a few minutes to write about your experiences in a journal each night creates the opportunity to review and learn from your day. It doesn't have to take a long time, but the benefits can be tremendous.

I start each entry with the day of the week, the date, the location, and the time. It looks like this:

**"Thursday, June 29th, West Yellowstone, MT 10:15 pm:
We went into the park today...."**

At the top of each page, I have the month and year. For the above entry, it would be "June 2022". After I had been journaling daily for a few years, I started alternating entries between blue and black ink, making the daily entries more distinguishable from each other, but those are just my

*Over the years I have written volumes of journals. If I had done this my whole life, there would be many more.*

preferences. The important thing is that you take a few minutes each evening and record the day's events, including what you thought about them and any feelings that came up.

Journaling will help you discover your purpose by helping you know yourself better. As you work on this milestone, I suggest you go for at least thirty days writing in a journal as you seek to discover your purpose.

## Go Screenless for Twenty-Four Hours

How easy or difficult would it be for you to go a full twenty-four hours without looking at a screen of any kind? I'm talking about computer monitors, TVs, tablets and yes, even cell phones. Most of us have become so connected to electronic devices that we might experience withdrawal symptoms without them.

Just as our bodies need sleep to recuperate and operate at our best every day, our minds need a break from the increasing barrage of attention-grabbing distractions. For most of us, going screenless for a twenty-four-hour period will be far more difficult than we think. Unless you go camping where there is no cellular service and you leave your phone at home, it may seem nearly impossible. Are you up for the challenge?

The point of this action is to help you disengage from all the distractions around you so that you can recalibrate your direction and priorities. It is difficult to learn your life's purpose if you are constantly distracted by the noise of mobile phones, social media, or video games. Pick a day when you have the best chance of success; a day when you're not required to be on a computer for work or school. Then leave your phone in a drawer on airplane mode or off for an entire twenty-four-hour period.

What the heck will you do for an entire day without a screen? Among other things, it will provide a great opportunity to take the next action I'm going to recommend.

## List Your Likes and Skills

Are there things you are especially good at? What do you like to do most? What things do you really dislike?

These questions will help you find your purpose. As you make this list, be as honest with yourself as you can. Some of the things you like to do might be the very things that distract you from finding and living your purpose. If you like to play sports or video games and you are good at them, that doesn't necessarily mean they should be your purpose in life.

Here are some additional questions to help you go deeper:

- Is there something you do that makes you feel good about yourself after you have done it?
- What difficult thing(s) do you feel like you should do but don't want to?
- What is standing in the way of what you think your purpose might be?

Take time now and write down the answers to those questions below. This will help you determine your current purpose. Give it some thought and see what you come up with. Use your journal if you need more space.

**What activities do I enjoy doing?**

_____

_____

_____

_____

_____

**What activities or skills am I good at doing?**

_____

_____

_____

_____

_____

**What have I done that was difficult or uncomfortable at the time but, when finished, left me feeling very satisfied?**

_____

_____

_____

_____

_____

**What do I feel like I should be doing but I keep procrastinating?**

_____

_____

_____

_____

_____

**Where do I want to be and what do I want to have accomplished five years from now?**

_____

_____

_____

_____

_____

_____

**Where do I want to be and what do I want to have accomplished ten years from now?**

_____

_____

_____

_____

_____

_____

**Where do I want to be and what do I want to have accomplished twenty years from now?**

_____

_____

_____

_____

_____

**If there were anything standing in the way of me living my purpose more fully, what would it be?**

_____

_____

_____

_____

**Write Your Purpose**

In the 11th grade, I was put in an advanced placement (AP) English class. I also had AP Calculus and AP Physics. It was hard! It required a lot of self-discipline that I didn't feel I had. I pled my case to my mom, who gave in and wrote me a note giving me permission to drop my AP English class. I had to get the note signed by the guidance counselor and by my teacher, Ms. Haltiner. I got the school counselor's signature, and then went in to see Ms. Haltiner. I told her, rather sheepishly, that I felt the workload from the three AP classes, along with the work I had to do from my other classes, was too much for me and that I had chosen to drop AP English. Ms. Haltiner sat down with me and said, "I'll sign the note, but I want you to tell me why you're dropping this class."

I don't remember what I said. She signed the note and I left.

I felt bad about my decision, but I knew I didn't want to have three AP classes anymore. It was a hard load. I left Ms. Haltiner's classroom with all the needed signatures to change my schedule to a regular English class and not have the extra burden. However, I didn't turn the paper in right away.

I went home and thought about it. That evening, I talked to a man I knew in my neighborhood who I respected. I knew he cared about what was best for me, not only now, but in the long run. He was kind enough to listen to me share my dilemma. Then he told me, "Don't drop the class." This man was a friend of our family, and I knew he had my long-term interests at heart. He knew and trusted my abilities better than I did. With his encouragement, I threw the note away and stayed with all three of my AP classes.

As you are thinking about what your present purpose in life might be, don't be afraid because it may seem hard, or something you don't want to do, or something that you are not yet good at doing. Just be honest with yourself and listen to your feelings and thoughts. When you're honest with yourself, you will know if what you are doing is something different from what you should be doing.

You don't have to pick a huge, when-I'm-seventy-years-old-this-is-what-I-will-have-accomplished purpose. Just look at the next five years.

Where do you want to be then? Where do you think you should be then? Make a conscious decision and then plan for how you're going to get there.

When you are living your purpose, you will be happier than someone who is just going through life doing whatever they want—with no purpose.

Having gone through these exercises, take a minute now and write down your current purpose. Remember, I said "current" because your life will unfold in phases. Your purpose may change over time as you develop and grow and as your circumstances change. Use whatever time horizon seems best to you now (one year, five years, twenty years, etc.) but take a moment now to define what you believe your purpose is and write it down:

**My purpose is:**

_____

_____

_____

_____

_____

_____

_____

_____

_____

_____

_____

_____

_____

_____

_____

_____

_____

# Purpose Path—Milestone #13: "Discover Your Purpose" Actions

| Action | Date Completed | Explanation | Examples/ Options |
|---|---|---|---|
| Keep a journal every day for 30 days | | Begin each entry with the day of the week, the date, your location, and the time of day when you are writing. For example, Thursday, June 29<u>th</u>, West Yellowstone, MT 10:15 p.m. (I like to underline my headings) Then write about what you did that day and what you thought and felt about it. | • Find a simple composition notebook<br>• Buy a formal journal<br>• Use a pen and paper, not an electronic device |
| Do not use an electronic screen for 24 hours | | Going without a screen for 24 hours will give your mind a chance to recalibrate without distractions. We're not just talking airplane mode. Keep your phone, computer, TV, and any other screen away from you (or you away from them) for a 24-hour period. Try this once a week for 4 weeks. | • Give your phone to someone else<br>• If work or school require you to work at a computer, pick a day of the week when you're not working or in school<br>• Find a good book and read it<br>• Play board games with family or friends<br>• Review your week |
| List your likes and skills | | Answer the questions above to gain a better understanding of yourself, including what you like and don't like. This can be one of the things you do on a screenless day. It is good to do this as you are about to complete the next action. | • Use the space in this book to answer the questions about your likes, skills, where you see yourself in the future, etc. |
| Write your purpose | | Whether you are working on your life's purpose or your purpose for the next 6 months, pick an appropriate time horizon and record your current purpose. | • e.g., "My current purpose is to help young men growing up without a dad gain confidence and realize that they can succeed as adult men today." |

## Record your experiences, thoughts, and feelings about this section here.

_____

_____

_____

_____

_____

_____

_____

_____

_____

_____

_____

# Milestone #14: Improve Yourself

To successfully live your purpose, you need to increase your capacity. What does that mean?

Earlier, I wrote about running with my son, Wesley. He was accustomed to it, and I was not. I had to run a little and then walk. Then I could run a little more, and then I'd have to walk some more until, eventually, I was able to run without stopping.

I was increasing my capacity.

Start with what you can do and work your way up.

When you take a class in school, do you try to take the easiest classes, or those that will be most valuable and stretch your abilities? You don't have to be the brainiac in the group, but don't just take the easy way out, either.

If you want to successfully grow into manhood, then you will need to increase the amount of responsibility that you shoulder in life.

You can set down the load you may be asked to carry sometimes. We all need a rest. However, being a successful man in many ways is synonymous with being responsible. Especially when it comes to being a husband and father.

I'm writing this book to you because I've been through what you are facing. We seem to have a growing population of adult men who aren't able, or don't choose, to shoulder increasing responsibilities. Some of these men may not have had a father or father figure to help them learn to become a responsible adult. Some men are afraid because they think they will fail, so they don't try. Some men followed the wrong crowd and are now suffering because of it. They never learned their "purpose." Don't let this be you. If it is, then know that it doesn't have to be that way anymore.

To have a fulfilling life, you need to be able to gradually increase the amount of responsibility you bear. So, what can you do to increase your capacity? This is what the world often refers to as personal development.

Remember how my weed-whacker seemed to function best when it was digging into its intended work? The next time you use or hear a weed-whacker, remember that you, like it, will be happiest when you are doing what you are intended to do. When you are responsibly living your purpose, you will feel the most satisfaction and fulfillment in life.

Here are four things you can do to improve yourself and increase your capacity:

**Read a Self-Help Book**

In an earlier action you were asked to read a book. There are so many books available from talented authors with engaging stories that reading can become addictive. It's a very good addiction.

As you seek to improve your abilities, you will want to include self-help or personal development books. I've got good news for you. Reading this book counts for this action.

In addition to reading this book, identify a skill that you want to improve, look for a book about improving in that area, and then read or listen to it (I often do both). When your body is busy and your mind is not, listening to recorded self-help books is a great way to double the value of your time. Working around the house, doing yard work, or exercising are great opportunities to listen to self-help audiobooks.

**Learn to Play an Instrument**

When I was in grade school, my mother encouraged me and my siblings to learn to play an instrument. In our home, it was either the guitar or the piano, though I believe my brother Scott played the tuba in the school orchestra.

Once a week after school, my brother and I would walk to our piano teacher's house, and we would each have a thirty-minute piano lesson. I remember practicing the piano while Mom was working in the kitchen fixing dinner. When I hit a wrong note, she would call out to me which note was wrong and which note I needed to play.

I didn't like practicing, but as I improved, I started enjoying playing the songs I was learning. I recorded myself playing the songs I had learned on cassette tapes. I don't think any of them have survived to the present day, but the thought of playing the piano for an audience spurred me on to keep practicing. I never did become a virtuoso performer. Today, I only play for myself once in a while, but the benefits of having learned to play an instrument are still mine.

It may not make a lot of sense to you at this point, but the next action on the Map to Manhood is to learn to play an instrument. Reading music, understanding music theory and principles, and being able to play an instrument help your brain develop in ways that it wouldn't otherwise. You can include your voice as an instrument if you choose to develop your ability to sing. If you do, you'll still need to read music as part of this milestone.

You don't have to become a maestro, but what you'll get from this is a window into your own capacity and ability, whether you succeed at your chosen instrument or not. This will take persistent effort, but it's worth it.

## Practice a Skill

My friend Danny and I started playing tennis at the courts in a park not far from where we lived. We played regularly. At first, we were lucky to hit the ball back and forth a few times before we hit it out of play. Over time, we got better. Eventually we got to where we could have a good set or two of tennis.

One night, one of my classmates, one of the cool kids who didn't hang around me much, rode up on his bike. He sat on his bike, holding on to the fence, just watching me and Danny play tennis. One particular volley was quite competitive. We both hit the ball in hard-to-return spots, but both managed to get to the ball and hit it back. I felt added pressure to do well, knowing I was being watched. Perhaps that helped me play my best.

I finally managed to hit the ball where Danny wasn't able to return it, winning the volley. My bicycle classmate was impressed. I knew because he said my last name in a tone that conveyed respect. "Stephenson." Then he rode off.

Whenever you begin a new sport, hobby, or activity, don't expect to be as good as someone who has been doing it for a long time. Improvement requires practice.

Whether you want to learn a new sport, or develop the ability to paint pictures, draw, weld, do woodworking, or whatever, you'll improve much faster if you practice deliberately. This is true for sports as well as trade skills. Choose a skill that you would like to develop, make a plan to practice that skill, and then follow through on the plan. Get help from those who are good at it. If it is something you can practice daily, then do it daily for five days a week, keeping track of how you're doing. Every increase in your ability will also increase your self-confidence.

## Review Your Journal

At one point in my life, I realized I was overweight. I had thought weight gain was an inevitable part of growing older, until I heard some people talking about it as though that wasn't true. It sounds so obvious now, but I realized that I could lose weight if I chose to live a healthier, more nutritious lifestyle. So, I started tracking my calories and exercising and I started to lose weight.

I didn't suddenly drop twenty pounds. It took a while. From day to day there was no visible difference. A half a pound on the scale doesn't represent a visible change in the waistline. I could see the lower numbers on the scale and that gave me encouragement, but the weight loss wasn't obvious to anyone around me at first.

At the time, I worked four or five days a week at one location, and a day or so a week at a different location. The people I worked with who only saw me occasionally noticed before anyone else that I was losing weight. There was a visible difference if you only saw me every other week, or maybe even once a month.

As you're going through life, you won't notice differences in yourself from day to day. One of the ways you will see the differences is by reviewing your journals.

A few years ago, I started going camping in the mountains—where there is no cell service—for four days each spring. I would take my journals from the previous year and review them. I would use the opportunity to assess my growth and development (or lack thereof). I would also set or recalibrate my direction for the coming year.

When I started doing this, I realized that you don't journal so other people will know what you did and what you thought. You journal so that you can see how you have grown.

Keeping a journal and reviewing it periodically serves to keep you from straying from your life's purpose. It helps you see yourself more accurately. It also helps you improve by learning from your most valuable teacher—your own experiences.

*A selfie while on one of my journal review camping trips.*

## Find Your Purpose—Milestone #14: "Improve Yourself" Actions

| Action | Date Completed | Explanation | Examples/ Options |
|---|---|---|---|
| Read a self-improvement book | | Find a book about something you want to improve in and read (or listen) to it. (Note: this book counts for this section. 12). | • Map to Manhood<br>• Find a book related to your current life's purpose |
| Start learning to play a musical instrument. Practice for at least 4 months. | Instrument:<br>_____<br>Start date:<br>_____<br>Completion date:<br>_____ | Choose an instrument; acquire one (used is okay, as long as it is in good shape. Rent if needed); find a teacher and take weekly lessons.<br><br>Practice every day for 30 minutes, at least 5 days per week. (More is okay.) Do this for at least 4 months. | • Guitar<br>• Drums<br>• Piano<br>• Violin<br>• Saxophone<br>• Cello<br>• Trumpet<br>• Voice |
| Practice a non-musical skill | | This could be a hobby or a trade-type skill. It needs to be something you can practice daily (5x/week). Consider taking up a new sport or activity – from tennis to chess – and then practice it for at least 6 weeks. | • Sports-related skills<br>• Household repairs/ maintenance<br>• Computer programming<br>• Chess<br>• Painting |
| Review your journals | | Here is a good schedule to use for journal reviews and reflection:<br><br>Daily – 5 minutes<br>Weekly – 30 minutes<br>Monthly – 2 hours<br>Quarterly – 0.5 – 1 day<br>Annually – 3–5 days<br><br>Use the time to read all that you've written along with your thoughts and feelings about what has happened. Using this review, look forward to the next week, month or year and plan using the lessons from your review. | • Nightly as part of journaling<br>• A weekly review/ planning session Saturday or Sunday evening<br>• A semi-annual or annual outing with limited distractions and connectivity |

# Record your experiences, thoughts, and feelings about this section here.

_____

_____

_____

_____

_____

_____

_____

_____

_____

_____

## Milestone #15: Live Your Purpose

Congratulations on getting this far on your journey! I hope you already have seen many benefits because of what you have done while working through this book. How can you take what you've done so far and make a difference in your life? Keep doing what you're here to do. Live your purpose.

So far on the Purpose path, you have completed exercises to help find your current purpose in life. It may be for the next six months or the next year or two, but for now, it feels like it's the main thing you should be focusing on.

This milestone will help you start living your purpose. Here are four actions that will help you to progress:

1. Set and achieve a personal goal.
2. Make a plan for your future.
3. Play your instrument for someone else.
4. Achieve three of the goals you have set.

### Set and Achieve a Goal

If you don't know where you're going, who knows where you'll end up? Fortunately for you, you do know where you're going. It comes from knowing your purpose. Having specific goals to help you accomplish that purpose will accelerate your progress. So, how do you go about setting goals? It's as easy as this: decide what you want and write it down.

As an example, my current purpose in life is to help young men who have grown up without a dad. One of the ways I can do that is by sharing my experiences growing up without my dad and the lessons I learned through that experience. I can do that by writing this book. For a more detailed explanation of setting and achieving goals, reference my previous book, "Small Steps, Big Feat" (www.smallstepsbigfeat.com).

I have a goal to publish this book. If you're reading it now, that means I accomplished that goal.

What is the most important goal you could set for yourself right now? Look at your purpose and ask, "What can I do that will help me accomplish my purpose?" Write that here:

_____

_____

_____

_____

## Make a Plan

Once you have defined a goal you need to determine how to make it happen. Making a plan will help you get where you want to be.

In the previous milestone, you chose an instrument to learn. If we use this as an example, then your plan could include practicing for twenty to thirty minutes a day, five days per week. Getting formal instruction would be a good thing, too. If you don't have the money for private lessons, look for someone who already plays your instrument well. Ask him or her if they could help you get started. You could set a goal to learn to play a moderately difficult song, practice it so that you can play it well, and then perform it for someone.

As you make your plan, it will be helpful to include target completion dates. It might look something like this:

| Action Plan/Step: | Target Date | Actual Date |
|---|---|---|
| 1. Acquire my instrument | Next Saturday | |
| 2. Find a teacher | 2 weeks from now | |
| 3. Begin lessons | 3 weeks from now | |
| 4. Practice 20-30 minutes daily 5X/week | 3 weeks from now | |
| 5. Play a specific song for my friends | 3 months from now | |

Include specific target dates with your plan. The more precise you are, the higher your likelihood of success will be. Don't be too aggressive. You may find that starting small and making progress is better than aiming big and disappointing yourself if you don't achieve your big goals right away.

For your chosen goal, write your action plan here:

| Action Plan/Step: | Target Date | Actual Date |
|---|---|---|
| 1. | | |
| 2. | | |
| 3. | | |
| 4. | | |
| 5. | | |

**Play Your Instrument for an Audience**

You may be asking, "Why do you keep pushing me to play a musical instrument?" There are several reasons. Music activates different parts of the brain. Learning to read music, playing it on an instrument, becoming proficient, and then playing it for someone else facilitates personal growth. Even when you make a mistake in front of an audience, you learn how to deal with it emotionally. All of this will be lost if you don't ever try.

All our children have learned to play one or more instruments. Our oldest child, Laura, became quite good at the piano. Eventually, her neighborhood teacher told us, "I've brought her as far as I can. She needs to go to the next level." In her case, that meant getting a teacher at the local college. During one recital at the college, she was playing a difficult piece on stage. She had done it well in practice many times. During the recital, she made a mistake, got stuck, and sat there with everyone watching her. As her dad, I could feel her anxiety and embarrassment. I was sending all the energy I could to her, hoping she would recover and not be too emotionally traumatized. After what seemed like minutes, but was probably only ten to fifteen seconds, her teacher, who was sitting in the front of the audience, called out, "Laura, just start where you can and keep going." That was enough encouragement for her to get her hands back on the keys, begin at some point in the piece and continue playing until she finished it.

Your audience might be just one person, but pick a musical number to play, learn to play it and then perform it for at least one other person.

## Complete Three Goals

After you have completed one of your goals, do it again. Then do it again. You'll get the taste of accomplishment. As you set goals aligned with your life's purpose, make plans, and accomplish them, you'll develop a pattern of action and growth for the rest of your life.

Complete at least three different goals that you set for yourself. Perhaps the most important part of this action is you will prove to yourself you can accomplish things you set out to achieve.

## Record your experiences, thoughts, and feelings about this section here.

_____

_____

_____

_____

_____

_____

_____

_____

_____

_____

## Find Your Purpose—Milestone #15: "Live Your Purpose" Actions

| Action | Date Completed | Explanation | Examples/ Options |
|---|---|---|---|
| Set and achieve a goal | | Considering your current purpose in life, choose a goal that will help you progress toward its fulfillment, and write it down. | • Learn a new skill<br>• Lose weight<br>• Become proficient at a musical instrument<br>• Learn a new language |
| Make a plan | | Plan the action steps necessary to achieve your goal. Write them down. Include target completion dates, and then act on those steps. | • Use the chart above or<br>• Write it in your journal |
| Perform a musical number on your instrument for an audience | | If you are taking music lessons, it is very likely your teacher will have a recital. This can be a chance to play your instrument for others. If not, find someone else, preferably several people at the same time, and play your instrument for them. | • Piano or musical recital<br>• Livestream yourself playing on social media<br>• Volunteer to play at an assisted living home<br>• The holiday season provides extra opportunities |
| Complete 3 separate defined goals that support your life's purpose. | | It is better to be focused on fewer goals than to spread yourself out over many goals. Pick the most important goal and do that first. You can work on more than one goal at a time, but seldom, if ever, should you have more than 3 goals you're working on simultaneously. | • Learn an instrument<br>• Lose weight/build muscle<br>• Read a book by a specific date<br>• Complete a degree or certificate program |

## Milestone #16: Enjoy the Journey

When I was in my first or second year of college, my life consisted of going to school, going to work, going home, and doing homework. I had fellow students and coworkers to interact with and friends to do some things with on

the weekends, but generally I was focusing on getting through college and paying my way as I went.

While at the student center one day, I noticed a sign advertising an upcoming dance. I thought it would be nice to go, and there was a particular young lady I thought about asking. At the time, I was living at home with my mother. She worked downtown and I sometimes drove her to work and then took the car up to the university campus. As we drove to her work one morning, I told her about the dance and the girl I was thinking of asking. I also expressed my concerns about the money for the date and the time away from study. When we pulled up to the curb, she turned and looked at me before getting out of the car, and said, "Jimmy, you've got to have some fun."

That was all the encouragement I needed. I thought of a creative way to ask this young lady to the dance, and she accepted. We went to dinner at a nice restaurant. (In fact, it was this date where I had the experience eating the peel-and-eat shrimp mentioned earlier.) We had an enjoyable evening out together – it was fun!

As you go through your journey of life, it is important that you take time to enjoy yourself.

### Have Fun Daily

As you go through your week, look for opportunities every day to do something just for fun. You don't have to spend money, so don't let a lack of finances stop you from looking for ways to do something just for fun.

Life is much better when you take some time to do something fun periodically.

What you think is fun may be different than what I think is fun. I like the outdoors and being in nature, but I recognize that's not everyone's cup of tea. However you define it, make sure you do something fun regularly. Every day, if possible.

List some of the things that you would consider fun to do below. Refer to your list when you feel the need for fun on any given day.

**Fun things I would like to do:**

_____   _____

_____   _____

_____   _____

_____   _____

_____   _____

_____   _____

_____   _____

_____   _____

## Go on a Trip or Outing

You have already had a family outing from Milestone #6; however, outings can be fun just for you. Usually, they are more fun with friends or family, but whether you go on a week-long vacation or an overnight getaway, an outing of some sort can be a great way to add enjoyment to life. Try for an overnight outing once every quarter. Do something you enjoy.

## Practice Gratitude

Gratitude has great benefits, not the least of which is that it helps us feel happier. When we focus on what we don't have, we create frustration for ourselves. If we manage to find a sympathetic listener when we complain, we may get some attention, but we won't feel better about our lives by complaining. When we learn to focus on what we do have, the growth we have experienced and the opportunities we can take advantage of, we see things differently. Learning to live in gratitude has a positive impact on how we see our lives.

Living "in gratitude" doesn't just happen. Like learning math or a sport, it can take practice. Chances are you won't have to look far to find someone who is worse off than you, which can help you feel better about your own life. But make it a habit to take a minute and be grateful for what you have, regardless of what other people are experiencing.

I saw a T-shirt recently that said, "Remember when you really wanted that thing that you now have?" It was a good reminder to be grateful for what we have.

As you journal each day, list at least three things that you are grateful for.

**Pay It Forward**

Do you remember Mark Gould? I told you about him in the introduction of this book. Mark was not a super-famous celebrity. He wasn't a successful businessman. He wasn't tremendously wealthy (though he seemed to be doing well from my perspective). But Mark had a good family. He had a good job. He gave of his time to help me and other young men in our neighborhood. He opened his home to me. He taught me things. He took me camping. Mark was doing something for me, not because I could pay him for it or because he expected something from me. He was helping a young man who needed his help, and he did it for no other reason than to do good.

The day will come for you when you are able to do something for someone else—perhaps another young man growing up without a dad. That time may be now. Don't forget to pay your successes forward. Help someone who is going through a challenge that you have experienced. Do it for no other reason than to help them. Show your gratitude by helping someone else. Do it often.

As you progress through your life, always take time to enjoy the journey by having fun every day, going on an occasional getaway, writing down what you are grateful for, and helping someone else while expecting nothing in return.

## Find Your Purpose—Milestone #16: "Enjoy the Journey" Actions

| Action | Date Completed | Explanation | Examples/ Options |
|---|---|---|---|
| Do something just for fun every day for 5 days | | Make a list of things you would do if you wanted to do something just for you. From that list, find those things you can do on a given day. Do at least one of those on 5 different days. | • Play a card game with a friend<br>• Go on a walk<br>• See a movie<br>• Eat out |
| Go on a trip or an overnight getaway | | I like to camp. Getting away from the city and into nature rejuvenates me.<br><br>You may not like to camp, but find a way to go on an overnight getaway with a friend, family member, or someone you enjoy. | • Go camping<br>• Stay at a Bed and Breakfast<br>• Stay at a relative's home<br>• Visit a national park<br>• Stay at a hotel or resort |
| Practice gratitude | | For 5 days in a row, at the end of each day, write down 3 things you are grateful for that day. | • Completed exercise commitment and it felt good<br>• Ate a delicious meal<br>• Had some fun with friends |
| Pay it forward | | Find someone going through a struggle that you have already been through. With the sole desire to help that person, help them. | • Help a younger sibling who is struggling<br>• Help tutor a classmate or younger student<br>• Write a letter of encouragement to someone struggling with a problem that you have already experienced |

**Record your experiences, thoughts, and feelings about this section here.**

_____

_____

_____

_____

_____

_____

_____

_____

_____

_____

> You become a man inch by inch and day by day
> as you take responsibility for yourself.
>
> You become more of a man as you learn to
> love yourself, not only so that you can be happier,
> but so that you can truly love others, too.

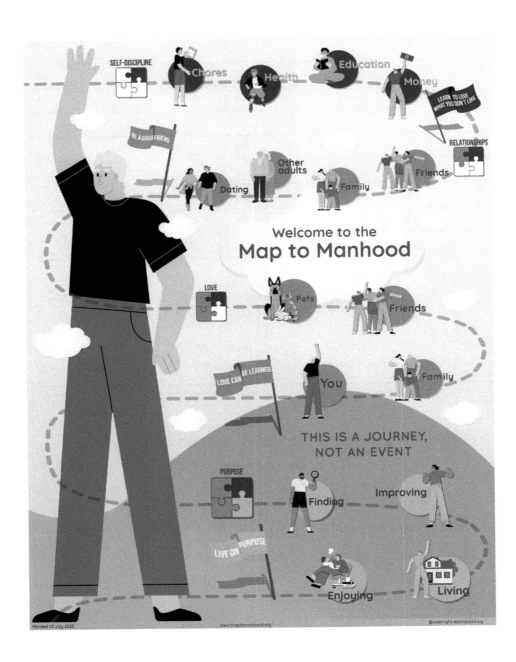

# Conclusion: Welcome to Manhood!

When I was in junior high school, I was enrolled in a metal shop class. Before we could go to work in the shop making things, we had to pass the book work. When we successfully completed our written assignments, we were given permission to put on a shop coat and safety glasses and go out and make things. When I got to that point, I entered the shop with my shop coat and safety glasses. I was one of the first ones done with the book work, so there weren't a lot of us out in the shop. I started to work on my first project at a worktable and the teacher, Mr. Jarrett, said to me, "You're in a man's world now."

You don't suddenly become a man when you turn eighteen or twenty-one. You don't become a man when some event happens to you.

You become a man inch by inch and day by day as you take responsibility for yourself. You become more of a man as you learn to love yourself, not only so that you can be happier, but so that you can truly love others, too.

You become a man when you have the courage to step outside of your comfort zone and do things that scare you. That might be standing up for someone who is being picked on or asking someone on a date. It might be taking classes that are more challenging in school or saying no to friends who are making bad decisions.

I hope the stories and advice in this book have given you insight and encouragement so that you can gain confidence in your ability to thrive as an adult man, husband, and father (if you choose), even though you may not have a good personal role model to follow.

The world needs you to be a good man. Your future family needs you to be a good man.

If I can do it, I have confidence that you can, too!

The choice is yours. If you choose to follow the map laid out with the milestones in this book, then, when you have sufficiently passed each milestone, I look forward to greeting you and saying, "Welcome to manhood!"

# Acknowledgments

I would like to thank the following individuals for their help and support in bringing this book to reality: Dr. Dung Trinh, for encouraging me to block out time and finish writing this book. For Susan Crossman, my editor and friend. This book is much better because of her thoughtful suggestions. Susie Schaefer of Finish the Book Publishing has been phenomenally supportive and tremendously helpful.

My wife, Suzanne (a.k.a. "Stepmom") has been along for a very uncertain ride in the years preceding the release of this book. I am grateful for her love and support. I am so much better as a man and a person because she married me more than thirty-two years ago.

In addition to Mark Gould, my "Stepdad," to whom this work is dedicated, there were other men who were tremendously helpful and positive influences in my teenage life; notably, Bill Cooley, and Steve Ballamis, Mark's neighbor, and son-in-law, respectively.

Finally, thank you to the hundreds of people who donated to help make this book a reality and to the thousands who have shared love and encouragement on the Stepdad social media channels. I hope you know that you really do have a dad who loves you!

# About the Author

Growing up without a dad in the home has challenges. James learned this firsthand, having been raised by a single mother as the youngest of five kids. Many challenges are practical in nature, but the deepest challenges are emotional. James wasn't aware of how significant those challenges were until well into adulthood.

While James was a teenager, there were a number of positive adult male role models that came into his life to fill the void of an absent father. One of them was Mark Gould. In many ways, Mark became a surrogate dad to James, opening his home, taking him camping, and even showing him how to ride a motorcycle and change the brakes on his mother's car.

To pay Mark's kindness forward, as well as others', James started a non-profit organization, a YouTube channel, and an Instagram page to help young men growing up without their dads. James and his wife Suzanne have raised five children of their own, all of whom are now adults.

Growing up in a single parent home, James has tremendous admiration and respect for those mothers who find themselves raising children by themselves. He also has deep empathy for kids growing up without a dad in their day-to-day lives.

Learn more at www.youtube com/c/MyStepdad or mystepdad.org

Milton Keynes UK
Ingram Content Group UK Ltd.
UKHW022027201023
431056UK00019B/184/J